WHATEVER HAPPENED AT FAIRFIELDS?

Whatever Happened at Fairfields?

SYDNEY PAULDEN

and

BILL HAWKINS

Gower Press

First published in Britain by Gower Press Limited
140 Great Portland Street, London W1N 5TA
1969

SBN 7161 0026 6

Set in 11 *on* 13 *point Garamond and printed by*
TONBRIDGE PRINTERS LTD
PEACH HALL WORKS, TONBRIDGE, KENT

Contents

Illustrations

Illustrations

Introduction

The Fairfields experiment was the centre of a controversy from the moment the idea arose in October 1965 until it melted into the Upper Clyde Shipbuilders merger in March 1968. It was a unique partnership between Government, private capital, management and trade unionists and there is much to learn from a study of how it came into being, what it achieved, and what the main actors think of their roles in retrospect. Britain so badly needs an answer to its problems of conflict between Government, unions and management, that any practical attempt to find an answer is worth recording and examining.

Bill Hawkins saw the whole story from the inside. He was seconded from the Thomson Organisation to help Iain Stewart before the experiment had begun. He became Executive Director, Publicity, at the new Fairfields yard, and, as the merger drew close, he was then seconded to Anthony Hepper during the formation of Upper Clyde Shipbuilders Limited, which embraced all the remaining yards on the upper reaches of the river. Hawkins was able to collect a mass of material, logging each stage of the complex story. He knew a book would have to be written.

Sydney Paulden is a freelance journalist and author. He came in to absorb Hawkins' material and carry out a wide range of new interviews with the key personalities. He could write the story as an outsider with no previous connection with Fairfields. He is, however, far from being aloof from the issues involved. He has made extensive tours of many foreign industries, including those of Japan, Germany and Sweden, and was the founder editor of an international shipbuilding journal.

During the research for this book, he became personally enthusiastic about the ideals represented by the experiment and keen to record the details before all the memories grew too dim. He also realised very quickly that it was much more than the story of a shipyard or an experiment in labour relations. It was simultaneously an exciting drama of power politics and business, spiced with the unorthodox behaviour of some of Britain's most piquant public personalities.

It should be stressed that where attitudes are criticised in the book, no attack is intended on the integrity of individuals. Every effort has been made to avoid entanglement in the personal feuds which have arisen from the Fairfields affair in Glasgow and in London. That side of the matter is left to the memoirs which will surely be published in the future. The authors' prime intention has been to give an answer to the question posed by so many industrialists, politicians, journalists and trade unionists: "Whatever happened at Fairfields?"

Chapter one

The £1 Million Stop-gap

Long-legged, mini-skirted Helen Jay walked round the shipyard to the cheering, whistling approval of 3000 men. Her mother, Mrs Peggy Jay, was to launch the biggest ship ever to be built on the upper Clyde. Her father, Right Honourable Douglas Jay, President of the Board of Trade, was to make a speech on behalf of the Labour Government.

The launching platform was unusually gay and crowded. Mrs Jay tapped a chisel-shaped fitting with a little mallet. This severed a cord and allowed the bottle of Champagne to swing down with a healthy crunch on to the glistening new ship. She named it *British Commodore*, all 67 000 tons of it.

There is always a nerve-wracking pause between the shattering of the bottle and the movement of the ship down towards the water. The striking of the mallet releases a switch which cuts off electro-magnets, leaving the hull free to heave itself down the slipway.

During the pause the yard's Productivity Director, Jim Houston, looked at the mark the wine had made and wondered again to himself: "Now is that the arse end of the ship or the pointed end?" It was the first launching he had ever witnessed and just a few moments earlier he had whispered to the yard's Chairman, Iain Stewart, "What are the chances of it floating?" "I wouldn't bet on it," said Stewart.

So open was the betting in Stewart's own mind that he

1

had two speeches prepared ready for the reception to follow the launching. In his left pocket was one to be delivered if *British Commodore* floated. In the right pocket was a speech to explain why his new venture was still not a failure even if the tanker capsized or sank when it hit the waters of the Clyde.

A lot depended on that moment. Besides the difficulties to be expected if a new company's first launching resulted in 67 000 tons of steel up-ended in the river, there was the problem of finance. The tanker was being built for British Petroleum and the owners were due to pay an initial instalment of £2 million as soon as the ship was launched. This would enable the new company to continue to pay its wages and put its new ideas into operation.

The Honourable Sir Maurice Bridgeman, KBE, Chairman of The British Petroleum Co Ltd, was on the platform with Lady Bridgeman. He was relieved to see the ship this far advanced, for not many weeks earlier *British Commodore* had been a tangle of bits of steel in a bankrupt yard, with doubts about whether or not its construction could be continued.

The only people on the platform who were unworried and able to enjoy the occasion were the shop stewards, union officials and workers' representatives and their wives. For the first time in British history the management of a shipyard had actually invited as guests to the launching a fully representative group of the men who had built the ship. Instead of being fenced off at a respectful distance from the top brass, they were there on equal terms, invited also to the banquet to be held that evening at Glasgow's Central Hotel.

Pat Kelly was there, the official Clydeside delegate of the Boilermaker's Society, the union which struck terror in the hearts of employers throughout the UK. Alex McGuinness was there, who had once thought himself blacklisted by management as the militant shop steward of the crane drivers. Alec Hill was there. Chief Timekeeper and Pay Clerk with the old firm, he had been on the staff of the Company Secretary and recalled that he met one of his bosses on business only twice during a period of about ten years, so wide had been the gap between men and senior management. These men had no doubts about the occasion because they had prepared scores of successful launchings and they were confident that their workmates knew how to build ships that would float.

They were just bewildered that it had taken so many years, centuries even, to be recognised as people with a part to play in making shipbuilding profitable.

British Commodore did float. It proved to the strange new management team of Fairfields (Glasgow) Ltd that they were now really in business, manufacturing ships.

The former owners of the yard, the Fairfield Shipbuilding and Engineering Company Limited, had come to an abrupt end ten months earlier. On 15 October 1965, at 4 15 on a Friday afternoon, a mere half an hour before the men were to leave work for the week-end, the yard manager had called to Alex McGuinness, Secretary of the Shop Stewards Committee.

"Come down, Alex, and collect the other shop stewards, too." When they gathered at his office they were simply told: "The yard is bankrupt. We are closing down."

It was not the practice of shop stewards to impart any news to the workers individually and there was no time to organise any meetings. The grapevine buzzed at the sudden call to a conference, but there were no facts for the men to bite on. They all went home to their families with nothing but rumours. It was the six o'clock news which told them they were losing their jobs.

They were not shocked at this treatment for there were no means of speedy communication between management and men. It was rare for any information of any kind to be announced voluntarily by the management to the workers. The surest form of communication which existed was the

3

grapevine leading from wives in the know to the local shopkeepers down to workers' wives and so to the men. This was how they picked up news about orders or possible redundancies.

The Shop Stewards Committee was able to make official applications to meet their bosses, but delays could be unbearable. A frequent procedure adopted by the stewards to force a confrontation was a "wildcat" strike. The men would down tools and march out of the main gates in a body.

The main purpose of this was to attract the attention of one of the shopkeepers in a neighbouring street. He was paid a retainer by a newspaper to grab the telephone as soon as there were signs of trouble at the yard. Within minutes the reporters would be on the spot and the evening headlines got the message through to the bosses that the men had to be met.

Although accustomed to a lack of information on matters which concerned their livelihoods, the Fairfield men were shocked to discover that the company had foundered with an order book worth £32 million and in the midst of a £5 million modernisation scheme. Fairfields was one of the most modern, best-equipped yards in the UK!

It seemed so ridiculous, that, at a big meeting on the following Monday, it was decided that they would not lightly follow the path of eight other Clyde yards which had gone out of existence in the previous five years.

On the south bank of the upper reaches of the river alone the 10 000-strong shipbuilding labour force had been slashed to 5000 and now 3000 more men were to be laid off. Out of the Simons Lobnitz yard, the Harland and Wolff Govan yard, Fairfield Shipbuilding and Engineering and Alexander Stephen and Sons, only Stephen's would remain, and for how long? The staple employment of the whole area for so many years was faced with total annihilation.

The Monday meeting was held jointly with the Fairfield-

Rowan Shop Stewards Committee. Fairfield-Rowan was the engine building division of the company, also threatened by the shut-down. It was forcefully recalled that over 60 per cent of any ship is supplied by sub-contractors outside the yard, so that scores of other engineering and manufacturing firms in the area would be hit by the closure.

As before on these occasions, the blow would also fall on tradesmen, shopkeepers, publicans, cinema operators and everyone dependent upon the revenue earned by the yards. Unemployment and a reduced standard of living would spread like a plague.

Alex Jamieson, Secretary of the Fairfield-Rowan Shop Stewards Committee, and Alex McGuinness, of the shipyard, started a campaign to alert everyone with any possible influence to the nightmare threat facing Govan, the district of Glasgow where the yard was located.

They aroused the support and the sympathy of Glasgow's Lord Provost Johnston, of reporters and producers at Scottish Television, at the BBC. They urged their union leaders to act at a national level. They harangued their Glasgow MPs and, through them, Government Ministers. They were prepared to fight until someone could be found to take over their yard and run it efficiently at a profit.

By one of history's strange and fortuitous combinations of circumstances, they had their wishes realised.

On the evening of 15 October 1965, a few hours after the stewards were told the yard was bankrupt, Glasgow's shipyard owners and industrialists were at the annual James Watt Dinner of the Institution of Engineers and Shipbuilders in Scotland. Iain Stewart, Chairman of Hall-Thermotank Limited and the immediate Past President of the Institution, was there. His office and some of his group's factories were in Govan, a stone's throw from the Fairfield yard. He had heard the news of the impending closure and was astonished to see the new President, Jim Lenaghan, Managing Director of Fairfield's, having to laugh, joke and act the life and soul of the party as Host Chairman of the James Watt Dinner. (Jim Lenaghan recounted later how distressing a situation he found this.)

For more than five years Stewart had cherished a dream of a new era of men-management relations. He had stressed in his Presidential Address to the Institution in 1961 that insecurity and inadequate information were the real causes of industrial conflict in Britain and had proposed a national scheme to remove fears of unemployment and of a lower standard of living from workers. He had known of the strength of these fears in the working population ever since he had been an apprentice engineer in his father's factory. He wanted the chance to prove that men and management could benefit from a policy of enlightened capitalism, with everyone believing in and enjoying the fruits of greater profitability. Eager to try out his ideals in practice, he had for some months been negotiating a scheme whereby workers who became redundant at Stephen's yard could be employed on specially generated city building projects created by Glasgow Corporation. The idea would be to train the men for two trades, so that they could be usefully employed on a secondary job during slack times in shipbuilding and still be able to provide an immediate work force to meet any new shipbuilding orders when times improved.

This type of retraining would contribute to increased efficiency in the yards and on the building sites, for the completion of a ship or a building project would not then automatically signify a period of unemployment.

It occurred to Stewart that the Fairfield yard could serve as a "heaven-sent" laboratory in which to put into operation many ideas on retraining, job interchangeability and new methods of internal communications which he felt sure could turn bankrupt yards into profitable enterprises, setting an example to the rest of British industry.

Jim Stephen, a member of the Stephen family which owned the neighbouring yard and with whom he had been negotiating the new project, was at the James Watt Dinner that same evening. Stewart approached Stephen and said: "Let's do it with Fairfields."

"Not Fairfields," said Stephen, taken aback. "Haven't you heard yet, it's bankrupt!"

"Ah, the vultures have already started collecting," was Stewart's reaction. When a yard went into liquidation, the other yards had cheap and easy pickings, of men and machines.

Meanwhile, the shop stewards continued to hurl bricks into stagnant waters and began to observe ripples. The following Friday, 22 October, Harold Wilson, Prime Minister, wrote to Richard Buchanan, Labour MP for Springburn, Glasgow:

> Dear Richard,
> Thank you for your letter of the 17 October about the Fairfield Shipyard. It is, as you say, a great disappointment that this yard which has done so much to modernise its equipment, has landed in financial difficulties. I was glad to see that the Official Receiver has said that he hopes that it will not be necessary to wind the company up and that meantime, it remains in business. The President of the Board of Trade has already seen Fairfield's management and is keeping in close touch with them.
>
> I entirely agree that the problem is to make the British shipbuilding industry as a whole more competitive in world markets. Last February we appointed a Shipbuilding Inquiry Committee, under Reay Geddes, to look into this. I have no doubt that they are considering points you raise about rationalisation and standardisation.
> Yours,
> *Harold Wilson*

On 1 November, Roy Mason, Minister of State (Shipping) at the Board of Trade, answered a letter from McGuinness and agreed to meet the Shop Stewards Committee during his forthcoming visit to Glasgow (Friday 5 November) to discuss the future of the Fairfield shipyard.

During that last week in October, John Rankin, MP for Govan, wrote in his weekly article for the *Scottish Co-operator*: "Now, in their hour of need, the people of Govan ask a Labour Government to stand by them.'

The Fairfield yard was in Rankin's own constituency and he was in very close touch with the two shop steward leaders, Jamieson and McGuinness.

One of them telephoned John Rankin at the House of Commons at seven o'clock one evening in the last days of October to inform him that £1 million was needed immediately to keep the yard open. It was claimed that this sum would give the men a breathing space, keeping their jobs for them until the whole issue had been thrashed out in more detail and some provision made for their future and the future of the yard.

The strong argument in favour of keeping the yard open was that the Geddes Committee, mentioned in Wilson's letter, was due to report early in 1966. It seemed logical to try to keep the yard in existence to see how its facilities might fit into any new concepts Geddes would propose. It seemed senseless to let this modern yard and its customer goodwill and its existing orders worth £32 million disappear just prior to the findings of an inquiry set up to "establish what changes are necessary in organisation, in the methods of production and any other factors affecting costs to make the shipbuilding industry competitive in world markets." Geddes might provide an answer to save the yard after it had been lost.

When he heard what sum was urgently required, John Rankin put down the telephone and walked immediately to the Chancellor's office in the House of Commons. Jim Callaghan was in.

"Jim," said John Rankin without ado, "I need £1 million." He explained the necessity of giving his constituents some small margin of room to manoeuvre.

"Where do you think I'll get it?" asked Callaghan.

"Well," answered Rankin, "you're the Chancellor. It's your job to know where to get money."

But this request fell on deaf ears. Callaghan held out no hint of a hope. Rankin then hurried to the central lobby and from there he dialled 10 Downing Street. The bell buzzed and a voice asked what he wanted.

"Is the PM available?" he asked in an irritable Glasgow accent.

"I am, John," said the voice, "Come over and tell me what's bothering you." So within twenty minutes of receiving the urgent message from the Glasgow stewards, Rankin was placing the facts before Wilson. At the end of a brief interview Wilson's answer raised Rankin's spirits to the roof.

"Don't worry, you'll have the money. Tell the men they'll have the money. Now go and see George, go and see George."

The news was phoned back to Glasgow from Number 10. There would be time to breathe. John Rankin did go to see George Brown, who was then First Secretary of State and Secretary of State for Economic Affairs. George Brown said: "Go and talk to Iain Stewart."

As a result of that promise from the Prime Minister, the Chancellor made a statement in the House, on Thursday 4 November, to the effect that the Government had requested the Bank of England to advance sums not exceeding £1 million to enable the yard to continue in operation. In his weekly article dated 13 November 1965, in the *Scottish Co-operator* (Rankin is a Co-operative Party nominee Member) Rankin said:

Kiss of life for Fairfield. . . . This is solely to keep the position open until the Chancellor and the

President of the Board of Trade have had an opportunity of exploring possible solutions to make the Fairfield yard viable and considering the findings of the Geddes Committee which will take account of this new development in its investigations.

Survival spells co-operation. This will entail a new form of management. The private yard is anomalous nowadays. If Government money is to sustain the industry, then Government representation on the management side is essential. Labour is just as necessary as finance. Therefore those engaged in building the ships must have a place also on the Board. The strike has to disappear from ship construction. It is too costly a weapon to use. The three elements in production are the men, the management and the money.

These words might have sounded like crying for the moon in November 1965, but, for a period of two years, they became a reality at Fairfields.

*   *   *

John Rankin took George Brown's advice and got in touch with Iain Stewart. When he was back in his Glasgow constituency for the weekend he telephoned Stewart and introduced himself. Rankin was accustomed to a pretty poor reception from the local industrialists who regarded him as a Red. Although MP for Govan for twenty years, he was not allowed inside the shipyards in his constituency. He used to stand at the gates and talk with the men as they came out if he had something to discuss with them. He had in fact been able to get into Fairfields officially for the previous three years by a stroke of luck, through getting friendly with another guest whilst on an invited tour of the river with the Clyde Trust. It turned out the other fellow was General Manager of the Fairfield yard. Having discovered

Rankin was a reasonable fellow, it was agreed he could enter Fairfields on regular visits.

"But," explains Rankin, "no member of the yard management would stand with me when I met the men. Wearing their bowler hats, the managers would stand twenty yards away, for they refused to mix with the workers."

John Rankin knew that Iain Stewart, in addition to being Chairman of Hall-Thermotank, was also on the Board of a list of major firms too long to recall, but including Babcock & Wilcox, The Dorchester Hotel Ltd, the Thomson Organisation, Eagle Star Insurance, the National Commercial Bank of Scotland and Scottish Television. He was, moreover, Chairman of the Royal and Ancient Golf Club of St Andrews and a member of the Governing Body of one of Scotland's most illustrious public schools, Loretto.

Knowing what little welcome he would get from the head of some other families, Rankin wondered what an Iain Stewart would say when he called. Iain Stewart said: "Where are you now? Right, I'll be at your door within twenty minutes." And a sand-and-sable Bentley took them back to Stewart's mansion at Bearsden for Sunday lunch. Stewart lost no time. In the car he began to relate the entire scope of the plans for Fairfield's future.

The exposition went on over lunch and through the afternoon. The idea would be a breakthrough for British industry, but for Glasgow shipbuilding it was a revolution.

The basic intention was to form a completely new company which would purchase the assets and orders in hand from the Fairfield Receiver. The capital for this would come from an unholy Trinity—the Government, the Unions and Private Investors. All three parties would take voting shares for their money, so that they became in effect partners in business. Each source of investment was to be represented on the Board, with Government and Union Directors, as well as Private Investment Directors and Executive Directors.

A brand new top management team would be introduced

to the yard from other industries, so that the latest management techniques could be brought to bear on the problem of building ships to a given time and to a given profit margin.

It did not need many words to convince anyone of the need for this new management approach, for the Clyde yards had considered themselves doing well to deliver a ship to its owners only four months late. In many cases deliveries were up to twelve months behind schedule. Heavy losses were being made on individual orders, so that the John Brown (Clydebank) yard lost an estimated £3 million on the liner *Kungsholm* built for a Scandinavian owner.

Fairfields made a loss of about £1 million on building the 7800 ton floating motel, the *Nili*, After the yard was eventually taken over, Stewart was to be met in New Zealand with a request for £602 000 compensation from the owners of the car ferry *Wahine* which, it was alleged, had been delivered nine months late and half a knot below specified speed capability. No wonder eight Clyde yards had been sunk without trace between June 1961 and January 1965!

In order to achieve an enormous increase in productivity, Stewart would demand a radical change in union and worker attitudes. Strikes would have to become an almost unknown rarity. Absenteeism and lateness would have to be cut to a fraction of the existing rate.

And, most critical of all the points in the plan, the unions' rule books would have to be drastically amended. In place of the strict demarcation between individual jobs there would have to be an agreed policy of "interchangeability" and "flexibility." These were words which had never in the past failed to raise the hackles of all the Clyde shop stewards. "One man, one job" had been the union war-cry for decades.

Stewart was confident he could raise the capital. His enthusiasm spread to John Rankin who became confident that the shipyard men would respond to this appeal.

"Give these men," he said, "a chance to do a job and they'll do it, and do it well."

12

Iain Stewart had no doubts about raising the cash, but he had set himself his own conditions. He would not go ahead with the scheme, he would not risk anyone else's capital nor his own time and energy, unless he had a firm and reliable promise of complete co-operation from the men at the yard. He knew that no management plans could succeed without this. The major task was to win the men over to his way of thinking, to the benefit of all concerned. He wanted to put his ideas to a mass meeting of the Fairfield workers, scheduled for Monday 13 December, and see if they would all pledge themselves to co-operate. However, it was not possible to organise such a meeting without the full assistance of the shop stewards of the yard and the engine works, so his first task was to persuade them to follow him.

He met the shop stewards, about seventy of them, in a back room of the Pearce Institute, a sort of club for the men alongside the Fairfield yard in Govan. Pearce had been the highly successful owner of the yard at the end of the nineteenth century. The room had been half-prepared for Christmas already, but there was no air of festivity when the stewards received Iain Stewart. His first words, when he came in, were: "I'm looking to you to rewrite the rule books."

Back came the immediate reply from their spokesman, Alex Jamieson: "Who do you think you are? Jesus Christ? I'm not fucking tearing them up for no one."

Stewart had a lot of explaining to do.

The men recall that he put their present plight into a historic and world-wide context. The working men were at war, against Germany and Japan, and there was even more at stake for them personally than in the two previous World Wars. Defeat this time meant unemployment and a loss of job opportunities for their sons. Once the yards closed down, they were gone for good. They would close down, almost all of them, as they well knew, unless something drastic was

13

achieved. They were fighting the battle for jobs and higher wages, a modern, bitter battle, with the bow-and-arrow weapons of a former age. The way to win was to use the modern weapons adopted so successfully in Japan, Germany and, above all, in Sweden. The civil war on the Clyde between men and management had to stop and the real enemy, foreign competition, had to be repelled by the latest industrial techniques, by total commitment to making yards profitable. Profit was the only thing which could bring higher wages for the men and increased capital investment from outside. Stewart then outlined what he demanded from them and finished with the words: "These are my conditions, and if you don't like them, get someone else."

There was a silence when he had finished his exposition. Then a little man in the middle of the room, still wearing his cloth cap and an overcoat almost down to his ankles, reminding Stewart strongly of the typical "feed" for a stage comedian, broke the silence with: "The way I see it, we're at the crossroads. We can go this way," (he pointed with a thumb,) "or we can go that way," (another thumb). "Me, I'm going that way." He opted for one of the directions he had indicated, leaving Stewart completely perplexed as to what that signified. However, Stewart said, "I agree entirely" and suddenly all the stewards were repeating the same words, "I agree." They would organise a mass meeting so that he would have the opportunity to put his case to the men.

The first skirmish had ended in victory, but there was now to be bitter fighting for Fairfield on several vital, distinct fronts. The men in the yard had to be won over to unconditional support of the scheme. The unions had to be confronted at top level to gain their agreement with the changes to their rules and to persuade them to invest union money in the project. A number of shrewd private capitalists had to be sold the new Fairfields as a worthwhile investment. Some highly resistant Cabinet Ministers had to be pressurised into making a Socialist Government become a 50 per cent shareholder.

The suggested arrangement was condemned by the ship-yard owners as "propping up the weak in unfair competi-tion," by Tory MPs as "creeping nationalisation" and by the unions as "interference with our sacred rights." To many Labour supporters it seemed certain disaster to be publicly committed to a branch of industry which had proved itself so far from viable. It was very fortunate for Fairfields that the man who took up the cudgels on its behalf in the Govern-ment was George Brown.

Chapter two

George Brown
to the Rescue

On Tuesday 21 December 1965 four shop stewards from Govan met George Brown over drinks in the House of Commons. They were Alex Jamieson and his subconvener Charles Stewart from Fairfield-Rowan engine works and Alex McGuinness and his subconvener David Kane from the Fairfield yard.

Present were also Bruce Millan MP, W Hannan MP *and* John Rankin MP. The stewards were a delegation paid for by the Fairfield workers to find out what was going on in London. They were described in the press as "four angry men," but they were more worried than angry. Jamieson at a mass meeting the previous day had declared: "If they say we are going to shut, they are in for the biggest fight they have had in their lives. We will get the backing of every shipyard worker on Clydeside."

As Jamieson had explained, he wanted "... the Government to stop playing with us and give a guarantee whether the yard and the engine works are to stay open or shut. We have had enough dithering."

They stressed to George Brown the social urgency of the Fairfield problem, how unemployed men rot and become forgotten men.

16

"My dear boys," said George Brown, "I've had many sleepless nights worrying about the same problem."

As Minister at the head of the newly formed Department of Economic Affairs, he had been pushing forward with a brand new and ambitious regional policy to stem the trend to unemployment and build up a prosperous regional industry. The closure of a yard such as Fairfields would bash another hole in the fabric which would take a vast amount of effort to repair.

His interest in rescuing Fairfields was "to save a shipyard." As far as he was concerned the new company would have to prove that it could be a viable commercial proposition. It would have to "float ships." He believed that a different kind of commercial set-up could produce the essential commercial viability. But the commercial set-up he desired had so far escaped him.

"Three times we built it up and three times all the arrangements fell apart," he was to comment later. "Finally it was pieced together again in a friend's dining room."

As will be seen, his efforts to create the new Fairfields were the cause of a feud with Roy Thomson which broke into the limelight nearly two years later with the public outburst which so puzzled the press at the time. He even went over the brink of resigning from the position of Deputy Prime Minister in that friend's dining room, retracted some few moments later when a solution to an immense obstacle was suddenly presented.

The main factor which contributed to the disappointments and failures of that time was the speed with which the arrangements had to be finalised. Brown had readily concurred in the guaranteeing of £1 million to keep the shipyard in operation until Geddes had reported, but it soon became apparent that a yard and an engine works with over 5000 men engaged in fabricating steel, building engines, installing machinery and fitting-out cabins could not survive much above six weeks with £1 million. Not only would it be necessary to pump in more capital if the original amount were not to look foolishly, even irresponsibly, wasted, but who knew how long it would take for action to be generated by the Geddes Report when it appeared?

In the event, the Geddes Committee recommended mergers in March 1966 and the merger on the Upper Clyde could only be brought into being two years later. Geddes was never expected to be a magic wand to turn losses into profits overnight. It was simply a report to point the road to greater competitiveness. When the dust had settled after the thunderbolt bankruptcy announcement of Fairfield on 15 October 1965, when the initial cash had been donated to create the breathing space, it was clear that fundamental changes had to be made in the yard if it were to be kept alive to play a part in Britain's future and to continue to employ Glasgow men.

This is why Iain Stewart's letter of 19 November 1965 stimulated a telephoned reply from George Brown the day it was received. This is an extract of what Stewart wrote:

Rt Hon George Brown, PC MP
First Secretary of State & Minister
for Economic Affairs
Storey's Gate
London SW1   19 November 1965

Dear George,
In my view the situation presents a heaven sent opportunity to expose the deep problems of the industry and grasp the nettle of overmanning, demarcation and management problems. I told Derek that if the Government would be prepared to back an experimental project such as that covered in the notes which Jack Scamp already has, I would undertake to produce a profit on the Fair-

field balance sheet, certainly within five years and probably within three.

Politically, of course, the saving of Fairfield would have immense advantages, but quite apart from that, in my view it would be criminal at this stage to pass up such a golden opportunity to benefit not only shipbuilding, but industry across the board. One wonders why this should be the case when things are so bad at Fairfield, but, psychologically, the worst things are, the easier it will be to solve the problem.

Iain Stewart

As Brown could see, the risks were terrifying, but the rewards were worth fighting for—the saving of jobs for now and for the future, the saving of supporting industries, the strengthening of marginal constituencies for Labour in the neighbourhood, another plank on which to construct his new deal for the underprivileged regions of Britain, a chance to put to the test whether or not Britain could build ships profitably in the teeth of foreign competition which threatened to wipe out the whole industry.

Stewart's letter had not arrived just out of the blue. His ideas and Brown's search for a solution to the Fairfield dilemma had been fitted together, painstakingly, and with the utmost tact (considering he was sandwiched between two forceful personalities) by an essential third man.

The "Derek" of the letter is someone with a strong claim to paternity over the Fairfield brainchild—Derek Palmar, a city merchant banker, now a partner in Hill Samuel & Co Ltd. In 1965 he was seconded to Brown's DEA from Philip Hill, Higginson, Erlanger's where he had been the expert on takeovers and mergers. He represented City interests and opinions on Brown's high-powered economic affairs committee.

He entered the Fairfield scene when he learned with dis-

belief that the Treasury had agreed to hand over £1 million
to the yard's Receiver without making enquiries.

"The most stupid thing!" was his immediate comment to
George Brown.

After an exchange of expletives with the Minister, he
argued that "If you are going to pour Government money
into the thing, at least the Government should have a shareholding."

Who but the Government, he reasoned, would be idiotic
enough to risk so much capital without having any say in
the way it would be handled and without having any chance
of profit for the risk it was taking?

It so happened that Derek Palmar had been Iain Stewart's
financial adviser for some years and the two had often discussed the basic problems of British industry together. He
became therefore the lightning conductor along which the
charges flowed, feeding Stewart's lofty management plans
into Brown's down-to-earth demands for a means to save
the yard's jobs.

It would have been impossible for a political outsider,
especially a member of the Tory Party such as Iain Stewart,
to implant such ideas into a Labour Government without the
help of an inside man. At the same time, an insider could
not have been successful without having a genuine belief in
the ideals, a responsibility towards the Minister and a raging
resentment at the unbusinesslike way public money could be
spent against all the rules cherished by the City.

Derek Palmar was in the perfect position to help, being a
merchant banker devoted to the private enterprise capitalist
system and simultaneously part of the DEA team to bring
Britain "screaming and kicking by the scruff of its neck into
the twentieth century," as Wilson had pledged.

It was Palmar who developed the formula of a fifty-
fifty partnership between Government and private investment. He sold Brown the idea of turning to Stewart to be
the Chairman of a new Fairfield company. He provided the

argument in favour of Government commitment in a more permanent rescue. The basis of this was the value of the Fairfield assets which should be preserved so that they could play a role in the new future to be outlined by Geddes, plus the opportunity to improve relations inside the shipbuilding industry.

Although the Treasury under Callaghan and at Wilson's bidding had coughed up the cash to save Fairfield from overnight closure, and although shipbuilding and shipping were the responsibility of Douglas Jay as President of the Board of Trade, the new Fairfield project became, as Palmar puts it, "the creature of the DEA." Once George Brown had accepted the formula, he took it up with gusto, added to it and battered through all difficulties and opposition.

Derek Palmar acknowledges that "it was entirely George Brown's strength that did it." It was George Brown who introduced the idea of Union participation in the investment, an idea which brought him a battle which was not won until almost ten months later.

George Brown was not just using a bedside manner when he told the four shop stewards on 21 December that he had had sleepless nights about saving their jobs. Between 11 October and 21 December he had pushed the Government so far along an unconventional path that his resignation would be the only answer if that path turned out to be a dead end.

And these had been the headlines on the morning of the twenty-first:

THIS SHAMEFUL SCUTTLE

Sometime this afternoon Economic Minister Mr George Brown is expected to announce in the House of Commons that the Government has abandoned any plans to keep Fairfields open.

It is a shameful—and totally unnecessary—decision. Gloom and despondency instead of hope

21

and cheerfulness will be cast over Govan this Christmastide. (*Daily Express*)

FAIRFIELD FAILURE EXPECTED
(*Scottish Daily Mail*)

BROWN'S BID TO SAVE FAIRFIELD
IS BEATEN
Big Business won't put up cash. (*Daily Record*)

During the afternoon of that same day, Tuesday, George Brown was obliged to make a holding statement in the House, in reply to a question for further information from John Rankin. The statement went:

> My Right Honourable Friend, the Chancellor of the Exchequer, announced to the House on 4 November the first step by the Government to try to save Fairfields yard from the very serious position into which it had been allowed to fall by the previous private owners.
>
> Since then the Government have been trying to establish the yard on a permanent basis. We have had consultations and negotiations with a number of groups. Despite the failure of some of these negotiations we have pressed on. Indeed, because I am still actively engaged in negotiations it would not help if I made a statement today.
>
> May I add that those who have charged the Government with indecision and delay should realise that the only decision which could have been taken promptly and effectively would have been to close the yard.
>
> It is because we have tried, and are still trying so hard to keep it going, that I hope to be able to make a statement tomorrow.

Behind the scenes George Brown had come a long way over many hurdles since receiving Iain Stewart's written offer to transform Fairfields into a profitable enterprise.

His immediate response had been to telephone to Stewart and discuss the whole project at length. Many discussions followed, with Stewart and with Derek Palmar. The formula was thrashed out for a fifty-fifty partnership (as Palmar points out, this was a partnership with the Government having *not more* than 50 per cent) and then sold to Government colleagues. A Cabinet Meeting on Tuesday 30 November agreed it in principle. It is believed that Brown had found a new ally in Callaghan, the Chancellor, by then.

The week prior to the Cabinet Meeting, on Tuesday 23 November, Callaghan was on his way to an 8 p.m. meeting with George Brown to discuss the implications of Fairfield and Stewart's letter. He was very sceptical about the whole affair. By chance, he went to an early evening cocktail party given by the Agent-General for Ontario Province, Jim Armstrong. During the party Armstrong came up to Callaghan and said, "Iain Stewart would like to meet you to talk about Fairfields." Callaghan left his group of friends immediately and so Stewart was able to meet him for the first time and give him a ten-minute intensive run-down on the whole scheme. Stewart pledged himself to bring in the private investors if the Government could put in their share. He emphasised how the scheme would be entirely dependent on the union's agreement to change their work practices so that management could manage without fetters. Callaghan went straight off to the meeting with Brown in a much less critical frame of mind.

Something of what transpired might be deduced from a letter which Jim Callaghan sent much later to Iain Stewart, on 16 January 1966, when the new company had actually been formed. This letter was hand-written and quite unsolicited:

11 Downing Street
16 January 1966

Dear Iain Stewart,

This is just to wish you good luck in your enterprise. You will need all your energy, determination, conviction and skill if you are to win through—becos you are facing scepticism and hostility—in many quarters—including from some where you have no reason to expect it.

I was a sceptic myself, but now the decision has been taken I wish you the best of fortune—because this can prove to be a most exciting new venture, that could open new vistas in shipbuilding.

Good luck,
Yours ever,
Jim Callaghan

The Government were now willing to participate in the venture, but were very dubious about the possibility of raising the private capital to back it with them. On 1 December, the day after the Cabinet's decision, the DEA officially invited Iain Stewart to be Chairman of the company it was hoped could be set up. Derek Palmar made the approach to Stewart before breakfast at the Dorchester, on behalf of the Ministry.

Stewart accepted. He stressed again, however, his conditions. The unions had to agree in advance to his new terms of work. The Fairfield men had to give an irrevocable pledge to adhere to new rules and promises.

Only two days later Stewart and Palmar were meeting with the members of the Scottish Trade Union Congress. Some of them had been subjected to a detailed exposition of his ideas in earlier weeks. On 12 October, just prior to the Fairfield bankruptcy, he had addressed seventy delegates from the unions in Glasgow whilst trying to start his job-

24

interchangeability scheme on Clydeside. The Secretary of the STUC, James Jack, had been treated to the Stewart philosophy in private conversation on several occasions. This time the matter was vitally urgent. Without immediate agreement Fairfields was doomed.

The STUC promised their support, on condition that Stewart gained approval also from the national union leaders. A meeting was therefore arranged with the national executives. They were able to organise it for Tuesday 7 December, still only one week since Brown had been given the go-ahead by the Cabinet.

Stewart arrived in London armed with statistics, a speech and his past writings. But this was George Brown's territory and within seven minutes he had explained and enthused sufficiently to get absolute agreement.

"It was a brilliant performance," Stewart was to say afterwards, "this was George Brown at his superb best."

Till this moment the plan and the negotiations had been under cover of secrecy. Nothing was to be announced until every thread had been securely tied round the package. There was still some way to go, especially to get the pledge from the men themselves and to find the private capital (around £500 000) to back the Government's.

However, once so many people had become involved, security became impossible. The news leaked out prematurely and hit the papers on the morning of 9 December. There were serious errors in the summing-up of the situation. It was wrongly assumed that as Stewart was Chairman of Hall-Thermotank and had been negotiating with the DEA, then the Government and Hall-Thermotank were making a joint take-over bid for Fairfield. Hall-Thermotank's shares dipped at the news.

George Brown was obliged to make his first holding statement on the issue that afternoon in the House. It caused quite a row and the Speaker had to intervene to shout, "Order! We cannot debate this in detail on a statement."

A full-scale debate had already been getting into its swing. Brown's statement went:

> In view of the leading part which shipbuilding plays in the Scottish economy, the fact that the Fairfield yard is an important and recently modernised part of this industry, and that the livelihood of many thousands is involved, the Government have been consulting with a number of interested parties to ascertain whether it is possible to establish the yard on a more permanent and satisfactory basis. These consultations are still continuing with some hope of success; but the Government have not yet taken any decision. The House will of course be informed as soon as a decision has been reached.

Anthony Barber, Opposition spokesman on economic affairs, jumped to the attack with three lengthy questions. His basic complaints were that the Shipbuilding Conference and the Shipbuilding Employers Federation had only heard of the scheme by chance and had not been able to meet the Minister.

Mr Barber was also worried that Fairfields, through Government intervention, might be placed in a privileged position *vis-à-vis* the privately owned yards.

"Finally," he asked, "why have the Government gone back on the statement made by the Chancellor of the Exchequer in the House on 4 November, when he indicated that a solution to the problem of Fairfields would await the findings of the Geddes Committee?"

Edward Taylor, Tory MP for Cathcart, Glasgow, formerly an employee of the Clyde Shipbuilders Association, also weighed in with questions on why the matter could not be left until Geddes reported in February and which Minister, Roy Mason (Shipping), Jim Callaghan (Treasury) or

George Brown (DEA), was conducting the negotiations.
George Brown came fighting back in reply:

> It is not a question of £1 million. I am afraid that
> private enterprise got itself into such a mess, and
> the banks—when he goes home this weekend, the
> hon. Gentleman might find out about this—helped
> to get it into such a mess, that there is not the
> slightest chance of this yard, left alone, carrying on
> until February or anything like February. If we are
> to keep the yard open, a yard which has been
> modernised at great cost, the Government must
> come in and see how they can help. This we are
> doing and I imagine that, when the hon. Gentle-
> man gets home, he will find that all Clydesiders,
> the people of Glasgow and most other Scottish
> people are rather glad about it.
>
> As to which Ministry is acting, the answer is
> that it is the Government as such. The fact that I
> am answering questions today indicates that, if
> people want to find one of us, I shall be ready to
> take the responsibility, but I am doing it in col-
> laboration with all my colleagues who are involved.

Following that tussle in the House, Iain Stewart came into
the open the same evening with a press statement. At least
one pressing consideration was the need to explain Hall-
Thermotank's position, to make it clear that the group had
no direct financial connection. Hall-Thermotank's shares had
been extremely sensitive during the previous five years. The
Thermotank part of the group, specialists in the manufacture of air conditioning equipment for marine installations,
had been founded by Iain Stewart's father and two uncles
in 1901. He had become the Chairman of Thermotank
Limited in 1950 and had steered the firm through a period
of rapid growth to a merger with J & E Hall Engineering

27

Limited, specialists in marine refrigeration, in 1959. The merged group had bought over Vent-Axia, the fan manufacturers, and gone public very successfully. Then, within a year, Stewart had had to resign from the chairmanship of the new public company because of the ill-health of his wife, whom the doctors had (wrongly) given only a few months to live. From 1960 to 1965, under the new top managers, Hall-Thermotank's shares slid from 18 shillings to below 4 shillings. Early in 1965 Stewart went back into the group as Chairman, paid off two senior executives with £50 000, and got stuck into the mammoth task of resurrecting the group's fortunes. And his own personal fortune, for, with 3 000 000 shares, he stood to lose well over £2 million. He could hardly afford to let his Fairfields project upset the efforts which were bringing Hall-Thermotank's shares rapidly back to health.

Stewart's press statement regretted the rumours and confusion, but explained that his lips had been sealed until an announcement had been made in the House of Commons. He confirmed he had been asked to become the head of a new enterprise which could be set up and that he would accept:

> ... on the assumption that the Government succeed in setting up such an enterprise and on the understanding that the unions would give their unreserved co-operation to the management in introducing flexibility and interchangeability between the trades at Fairfields.
>
> Broadly speaking this means that the management would have complete freedom to introduce a variety of new techniques. Fairfields would become a proving ground for new ideas, new methods, and the elimination of unnecessary practices if the plan is acceptable.
>
> These measures, I believe, would not only re-

establish the company as a commercially viable unit but would also enable the men to share in the prosperity which can be achieved by proved productivity performance.

This was the first time that Fairfields was publicly put forward as a kind of "industrial laboratory" (as it came to be known) to experiment with new approaches to better men-management relations and to improved productivity.

The next day, Friday 10 December, there was a mass meeting of 5000 men and union officials in the Lyceum Cinema, just along the road from the Fairfield shipyard. The meeting was held in secret with entry barred to reporters and other outsiders. George Brown and Iain Stewart had, however, left little to chance, having now primed the shop stewards committees, the Scottish delegates and the national leaders.

Chairman of the meeting was the late Harry Gallagher, Chairman of the Clyde District Committee of the Confederation of Shipbuilding and Engineering Unions. The principle speaker was John Chalmers, Scottish executive member of the Boilermakers. James Jack, General Secretary of the STUC attended with his Chairman, Alex Kitson. These had all been spoken to at length by either George Brown or Stewart or both.

Tough, bespectacled Harry Gallagher did not mince his words. "This is the end of the road for Fairfields," he said. "You either agree to interchangeability or lose your jobs."

The men voted overwhelmingly to follow Brown and Stewart. Plans were made for Iain Stewart himself to address a similar mass meeting on the following Monday, 13 December, to give them his plans in detail. But that big event did not take place. George Brown bawled Stewart out over the telephone for moving too quickly with the men before the cash problem had been settled. The big plum private investors were not coming in as hoped and there were major obstacles preventing the unions from taking a financial interest in the new set-up. Stewart was ordered to cancel the Monday meeting and to keep his mouth shut. Brown's position was becoming uncomfortable, not to mention Stewart's.

Chapter three

The Millionaires' Round-up

Lord Fraser, the late chief of the House of Fraser, a neighbour and friend of Iain Stewart, was the first to indicate he could come in with cash to back the new Fairfields company. As a very patriotic Scottish businessman, he said he would throw £100 000 into the kitty as soon as an acceptable consortium had been organised.

Lord Fraser was also the first to climb out. He withdrew when he heard that Lord Thomson was in. An old hostility counted for more than a new enthusiasm. This is how the antagonism had arisen. Another close friend and neighbour of Lord Fraser was Jim Coltart, Roy Thomson's Deputy Chairman. Coltart and Stewart were also colleagues on the Board of Scottish Television Limited (of which they are now Chairman and Deputy Chairman respectively), and on the Board of Thomson Organisation Limited. The three Glasgow tycoons, Fraser, Coltart and Stewart, had had tea regularly at Fraser's house for almost three years. Their major topic for discussion had been a merger between *The Scotsman*, which was Thomson's morning newspaper published in Edinburgh, and *The Glasgow Herald*, published by Outram's, of which Hugh Fraser was Chairman.

All were agreed on the advantages of such a merger, for there were many areas where rationalisation would be obvious

31

and profitable. Many services, such as London offices, Glasgow and Edinburgh branches, were duplicated, and the same applied to the two evening papers, *Edinburgh Evening News* and Glasgow's *Evening Times*, each a sister to the morning papers. Fraser was warm to the idea of a merger, but insisted that there had to be no hint of a takeover. He probably knew something not previously disclosed, that ten years previously Thomson had had a bid for Outram's already printed and ready for dispatch to Outram shareholders when, the afternoon prior to the posting, Lord Kemsley had telephoned Thomson to reopen negotiations which led to Thomson's acquisition of Kemsley Newspapers. The bid for Outram's had been cancelled at the last minute, for Thomson realised he would first have to digest the Kemsley empire before he could take another big bite at British newspaper publishing.

The later discussions with Fraser dragged on interminably, with Fraser always ending with, "I'll think about it, I'll let you know." He may well have been playing with his two friends in this way in order to stave off an outright bid. However, their patience exhausted, Thomson's prepared and printed an offer once again. The day before this one was to be posted, Coltart asked Roy Thomson if he could be allowed to make one last approach to Fraser on the partnership terms previously discussed. Learning that Fraser was flying via London on his way back to Glasgow from Monte Carlo, Coltart collared him on the afternoon plane and arranged a meeting for that evening without disclosing his reasons. But when the two met at Fraser's house at 8 30 p.m., Fraser said: "Look, Jim, I'll write on this cigarette packet exactly what you are going to tell me before you begin. Just see if I'm right." When Coltart had explained his mission, Fraser handed over the Senior Service packet which bore the scribbled words: *"You have put an offer in for Outram."*

Coltart argued until 11 30 p.m. to try to persuade Fraser to let the bid become unnecessary by agreeing to the merger,

offering Fraser the promise of being the first Chairman of
the new partnership. Fraser would only say, "I'll think about
it between now and 9 30 tomorrow morning." Coltart ended
by telling his friend he was very despondent, because he was
sure that Fraser knew the merger was right for the papers
but was simply looking forward to the thought of a takeover battle with Roy Thomson. There was a bitter fight for
control of the *Glasgow Herald* and Hugh Fraser won. Shareholders of Outram's who lost 9 shillings per share in the
end due to the share exchange formula which gained Fraser
victory, were still content to say, "Ah, but we kept Thomson
out." The battle had apparently been basically to keep a
very Scottish property in Scottish hands. Many Scots still
resented the fact that their proud paper *The Scotsman* had
gone to a Canadian who had the effrontery to drive up to its
offices the first day in a huge garish Cadillac. As Thomson
himself put it: "In Edinburgh I was as popular as a skunk
at a tea party."

When Thomson made his bid for Fraser's papers, the
man he nominated to be Chairman if the bid succeeded was
Iain Stewart. He had been one of the few Scottish businessmen to rally to Thomson's side when Thomson was trying
to set up Scottish Television. At that time Thomson had
been extremely anxious to obtain prominent Scottish names
to support his plans, but Outram's, for example, much
earlier than the takeover battle, had refused to become associated, even when Thomson offered to lend them the money
to invest! Stewart's link with a "foreign" intruder on the
Scottish business scene must have contributed to the suspicion
with which his ideas for Fairfields were received in some
local business circles, just as his sons at Loreto were told by
the sons of other Scottish industrial family dynasties that
their father was "a traitor to his class."

The criss-cross of suspicion and accusation did not follow
any lines of logic on the plans put forward for Fairfields.
Stewart was in turn dubbed a "red," a "greedy capitalist," an

THE MILLIONAIRES' ROUND-UP

"MRA undercover agent," "traitor to Glasgow." Luckily, there were others who called him "true son of the city and a Scottish patriot," a "practical idealist" and a "man with the cure for the English sickness (of industrial inefficiency)." Roy Thomson agreed to invest in Fairfields because he was keen to see a start made with new labour relations in industry. His publishing empire had been plagued severely with restrictive practices. He saw that the Fairfield scheme could point the way towards improved management-union communications. Thomson was told that Fraser was in and had no objection just so long as it was Iain Stewart's show and not Fraser's, but, when this information was relayed to Fraser, out went Fraser.

Stewart had caught one and lost one, but luckily he had other fish to fry. On Sunday 12 December, he was reported in the press as confident of raising all the necessary cash privately if the Government failed to come in. He was in touch with two other wealthy Glasgow businessmen, Sir Isaac Wolfson, who still liked to think of himself as the Glasgow-boy made good, and Hugh Stenhouse, Chairman of Stenhouse (Holdings) Limited and of a number of substantial insurance and industrial undertakings. One other Scot, with the courage to take the plunge and place his money where his heart led, sat down and dashed off a handwritten note that Sunday. It landed on Stewart's desk on Monday 13 December, the depressing day of the cancelled mass meeting with the Fairfield workers. It said:

I am interested in your attempt to make Scottish Shipbuilding competitive with (say) that of Sweden, where labour relationships are so incomparably better. The less the Government is implicated, the greater would be my interest.

I would consider a personal investment of (say) £100 000.

Captain Harold Salvesen

34

A short time later the cheque for £100 000 arrived and it was in the bank whilst the hunt went on to find company for it. Captain Salvesen made it clear in his note that the cash would be from him personally and had nothing to do with the shipping line which he ran. It would seem likely that his action had been stimulated by material such as that in the *Sunday Mail* article by John Loch:

THIS MAN STEWART
This Fairfields business is the greatest chance Scotland has ever had. It could be the start of a whole new way of life for industry and the worker.

So the headline went, with a story beneath that included comments such as:

Twenty minutes in Iain Stewart's office is like twenty minutes of exhilaration on the Big Dipper. It's a vibrant experience with Stewart talking about high finance one minute and just as knowledgeably about the working man's distrust of high finance the next...

Stewart was quoted as saying:

Scotland's shipyards have the worst communication set-up I know when it comes to keeping the man on the shop floor informed...I don't for one minute blame the workers for being worried about what is happening to them...for being a bit reluctant to change their ideas. Their security is at stake and they are worried. I am out to give them real security if they will give me their confidence. Industry, to be a success, must be based on complete trust on both sides.

Fairfields is only a start. If we can succeed with new concepts, other industries will follow suit.

The Salvesen support out of the blue was refreshing for Iain Stewart, but he kept it secret. The First Secretary of State, George Brown, was working on the assumption that one single private investor would be found to equal the Government's shareholding. His eyes were fixed on Roy Thomson. Stewart, however, was firmly set, in his own mind, against such an equal balance between two investing parties. He wanted the Government's share to be no more than 50 per cent, as agreed, but he also wanted a syndicate of a number of investors, preferably including the unions, to provide the remaining capital. He wanted to feel free to act as bona fide Chairman of a really free Company, not as some kind of middleman reporting to two masters. He was keen on Government *money*, not Government *pressure* and he wanted Roy Thomson as a shareholder, not as a shipyard controller.

There were therefore serious possibilities of a misunderstanding when George Brown, Iain Stewart, Jim Coltart and Roy Thomson met, "secretly," to talk turkey. George Brown went over to Thomson House in Gray's Inn Road. The lift taking him up to the sixth floor stopped at each floor on the way, the automatic doors opening wide to give every passer-by a good view of his substantial presence.

"I thought these bloody talks were supposed to be secret," groaned Brown.

The talks went well. The four men exchanged ideas in the aesthetic environment of a suite of offices where the décor and furnishings had been specified by Lord Snowdon. At the end, as the Minister was leaving, Roy Thomson joked: "Shake hands with a fellow capitalist.' Brown left with spirits high, convinced that he had been given Thomson's word that the rest of the capital required would now be forthcoming. Astonishingly enough, after such detailed talks, this impression seems to have been a complete misunderstanding. Roy Thomson and Iain Stewart had been talking in terms of about £150 000, whilst George Brown had in his mind the figure of £500 000 to match the Government's. There was therefore a volcanic reaction from George Brown when he received confirmation of the smaller sum. He attacked Thomson ferociously on the telephone, to such an extent that Thomson wanted to withdraw from the whole deal. This further enraged Brown who was now convinced that he had been led up the garden path by "a cheat." When Thomson visited Brown's offices, accompanied by Jim Coltart, Harry Henry and Gordon Brunton, his top executives, to sign the necessary share documents later, there was a terrifying row, in which Brown swore that Thomson had promised the half million and was now purely backing down because of the advice of his colleagues, "the faceless ones" as he called them to their faces. "You're not the boss," he taunted Roy Thomson, "you're the office boy. These other people tell you what to do."

This incident rankled and smouldered inside George Brown for more than a year until it burst into flame at that notorious dinner in the Savoy Hotel. The Westinghouse Corporation of America were holding one of their seminar weeks in the UK which culminated in a massive banquet. About one hundred of America's top businessmen were to attend and the Westinghouse Senior Vice President, Peter Scruth, approached his old friend Jim Coltart, to ask if the Thomson Organisation would like to act as joint hosts and invite some of their UK contacts. This was agreed and Roy Thomson was asked to Chair the banquet as the master host. Thomson's invited the heads of Britain's biggest industrial firms, such as Sir Frank Kearton of Courtauld's. However, before the approach to Coltart, Scruth had already sent an invitation to the Guest of Honour—George Brown. This was the setting at the Savoy when those transatlantic top people gathered for their junketing. During the meal, Roy Thomson asked Jim Coltart if he thought it would be a good idea to tell a certain corny joke and to use George Brown's name in the telling of it. Coltart thought there could

37

be no objection, but Brown overheard and warned them:
"No jokes with my name, or else I'll tell them all how you
cheated me."

"It's just in fun," Coltart laughed, but Brown was in
earnest.

"Fun or no fun, don't mention my name."

George Brown was at that time Foreign Minister. Coltart
remembers that Brown had had practically nothing to drink
the whole evening. Roy Thomson did mention George's
name in a corny joke in a speech and, when Brown stood
up to reply as Guest of Honour, he turned on his host and,
in front of the hall full of international business guests and
press reporters, he lambasted Thomson as "the only man
who ever broke his word to me, a man who is a cheat."
Brown was suffering from an intense feeling of resentment.
He was incensed.

Brown did not explain himself and, although the papers
were full of the incident, none seems to have come close
to its origin, except for *Private Eye* which did connect it
somehow with Fairfields. Most others confused it with a
disagreement over *The Sunday Times'* treatment of the
Philby spy story.

The Chairman-designate of the new Fairfields company,
if there was ever to be one after the Brown-Thomson rift,
had a tough task keeping Thomson in the scheme. Thomson
had never anyway been convinced of the security of the
investment, especially as it had not failed to catch his notice
that Charles Clore had lost to the tune of millions in another
British shipyard, Furness Shipbuilding Company in the north-
west of England (which eventually closed down in 1968).
Was idealism worth insults on top of a risk of £150 000?
Iain Stewart managed to convince Roy Thomson that it
was.

Sir Isaac Wolfson played a part at that juncture, even
though he was in mid-ocean on board *Windsor Castle* steam-
ing to South Africa. Jim Coltart got Isaac Wolfson on the

telephone and he agreed to take up £100 000 worth of shares if Roy Thomson was in. Roy said OK, he would stay in if Isaac came in. That situation was saved.

The cancellation of Stewart's intended address to the Fairfield workers caused dismay amongst the men and their unions. This developed into great suspicion and concern as the days passed without any concrete statement from the Government or Stewart. George Brown was fully occupied trying to chase in the cash to replace Thomson, whilst Stewart had had his lips sealed at the express order of the Minister.

At another mass meeting of Fairfield men on Monday 20 December, Alex Jamieson shouted that they were fed up with all the Government's dithering and the lack of progress. He maintained that they were still ready to accept changes but not on the basis of "grinding workers down into the ground." The earlier euphoric mood of co-operation was being dissipated by the delay. Tempers were rising on all sides.

"I think I'll bugger off to Canada," Roy Thomson told Stewart.

Opposition had also had time to become organised from the other shipbuilding yards, whose owners were hostile to any form of Government control over an individual yard. They feared that Government contracts would be handed over to its protégé on an unfair basis. On Friday 10 December a delegation from the Shipbuilding Conference and Shipbuilding Employers' Federation put an alternative plan for Fairfields to Roy Mason, Minister of State for Shipping at the Board of Trade. They learnt at that meeting that it was imperative to meet George Brown who was "running things."

The bosses' delegation, which included the Presidents of the Shipbuilding Conference and the Federation, continued their lobbying in London. Iain Stewart had a secret meeting with them and then, on Wednesday 15 December, they caught up with George Brown. There was a violent exchange of angry views. The shipbuilders had an alternative plan to offer in place of the Government sponsored takeover. They proposed to tide over the situation, until the Geddes Report, by assisting in the completion of work which was under way in Fairfields, making "every endeavour" to find alternative employment for the Fairfield men as they became progressively redundant.

As James Jack, Secretary of the Scottish TUC put it later, the shipbuilders "went into Fairfield in order to be grave-diggers for the firm." "Kill it painlessly," was how a leader in *The Scotsman* put it.

George Brown indignantly rejected the whole offer, but he was still far from reaching a solution along his own lines. The next day, Thursday the sixteenth, he was expected to make a complete statement in the House on the Fairfield rescue. Mr Bowden, Leader of the House, even rose at one point to explain that The First Secretary of State would be making a pronouncement a little later that afternoon. But Brown had nothing promising to impart and he did not appear. He was still hunting for the necessary financial backing. His search led him up many avenues which suddenly turned into cul-de-sacs.

The evening after the non-statement in the House, Max Stewart, Iain's nineteen-year-old son, answered the phone in the family home at Bearsden, Glasgow. It was George Brown calling.

"My father is out," Max explained.

"Where is he?"

"At a dinner and dance," Max said.

"What!" howled Brown, "He's gone dancing at a time like this!"

Iain Stewart's dancing (at a Scottish Television annual ball) was interrupted when his name was called over the loudspeaker in the ballroom. "Wanted on the telephone," he was told.

"Iain!" Brown shouted, trying to make Stewart hear over

the sound of the orchestra, "I've got Robert Maxwell and Harold Lever here with me! They can put up the money! Tell them all about it!"

Stewart had to dash by car to the Central Hotel where he could cram himself into an enclosed telephone cubicle and relate in detail in quieter surroundings all the facts and figures and hopes and risks and rewards of the Fairfield plan. At the end of one and a half hours, his body streaming with sweat from exertion and the stifling, claustrophobic atmosphere of the cubicle, Iain had told Maxwell and Lever enough to satisfy them. They were in.

But they were not allowed to stay in. Callaghan and Brown had a collision of views, Callaghan maintaining that a cash investment from two Labour MPs in addition to the Government's backing would unbalance the whole project and would be politically disastrous.

Brown would not agree and so the argument had to be taken further for a decision, to Harold Wilson. The Prime Minister was abroad at the time, seeking a solution to other problems, when Callaghan's request for an answer came through to him. Wilson came down on the Chancellor's side and Maxwell and Lever were counted out.

It was now only eight days to Christmas and there was no message of good cheer that the Government could give to the Fairfield men and to Clydeside.

However, Stewart had patched up Roy Thomson's feelings, Isaac Wolfson was following Thomson's lead and the union leaders had shown interest in staking some union cash in the project to keep the 3000 men's jobs open and to try out some new ideas of management. Brown had come round to the idea of a consortium of a number of private investors to match the Government shareholding.

Derek Palmar had been negotiating feverishly with Alex Mackenzie, the Fairfield Receiver, working out terms for purchasing the yard's assets. A figure of £1 million had been suggested and Palmar had recommended that share capital should be raised to cover that amount, with additional Government loans and guaranteed overdraft facilities to serve as the new company's working capital.

When the promises were totted up, including, of course, the £100 000 cheque from Captain Salvesen, Brown and Stewart felt they could go ahead and announce the formation of a new Fairfields if one more private investor could be found. Wednesday 22 December had been set as an absolute deadline for success or failure and the extra cash had to be raised by then, otherwise failure would have to be admitted.

There was no margin of error left now, for the original £1 million stop-gap plug from the Chancellor was gone. The Receiver had to make a move to offer the assets for sale piecemeal if no one came forward to take them as a whole and, once the Christmas recess hit Parliament, then final decisions would be too delayed to be effective. Some of the shipowners who had placed orders with Fairfields were anxious about the future of their ships and would have to transfer the orders to other yards if there were no definite announcement soon. It had to be by 22 December or never and already, as we have seen, the headlines were prophesying doom and the Fairfield shop stewards and men were preparing for an all-out fight to stave off the threatened closure. It was at this point that Brown could so truthfully confess to the four shop stewards, over beer in the House of Commons and in the company of the Glasgow MPs, "I've had many sleepless nights."

Although unable to make public pronouncements, Iain Stewart had not stopped selling his idea to individuals. He was already busy hunting the nucleus of a management team. Collecting the cash was only the start of his problem. Once founded, who was going to staff the new company and make it perform the miracles which so many commentators had mockingly referred to as Stewart's "dreams?"

At the beginning of December, when Stewart was returning to Glasgow after having been offered the position of Chairman-designate of a new Fairfields, Oliver Blanford arrived at London airport with time to spare for the flight he had booked. "There are plenty of seats on the earlier plane just about to leave," suggested the BEA receptionist, "why not catch that?"

Blanford made a dash for the plane but found when he reached it that he was stopped from turning into the tail-end compartment. He had a first-class ticket, but that flight was tourist class right through and the rear seats were already taken. The slight commotion at the entrance as he stated his case to the stewardess caught Iain Stewart's attention and he waved to Blanford from one of the rear seats. Stewart then kindly but firmly asked the man next to him if he would not mind moving further up the plane and made way for Blanford to sit next to him. They had only met a couple of times previously and Blanford had recognised Stewart's face but had not been able to put a name to it. Blanford was at that time General Manager of the Stephen's engineering works next door to the Fairfield yard and had been introducing work study, measured daywork and a number of advanced management techniques into the works where the main engines were built and then installed into the ships constructed by Stephen's yard. He was making great strides towards new peaks of productivity, but his one major complaint was that Jim Stephens, the boss, would not yet allow the new methods to be applied to the yard itself.

Stewart had been impressed by what Jim Stephen had earlier related about Blanford's activities during the previous negotiations over the interchangeability of labour between Stephen's yard, the Corporation building sites and Thermo-tank. He was therefore delighted to have the chance to discuss his Fairfield project with Oliver Blanford during their chance meeting on the plane. "What would you do to set the yard on its right path?" Stewart asked Blanford as the plane taxied towards the runway.

Blanford told him, during the one hour twenty minutes the plane was in the air. As the wheels touched down at Glasgow, Stewart asked, "Now, will you come and do all that for me?"

Blanford said he would be very happy to do so, but he was under contract to Stephen's. Still, they kept very closely in touch whilst the finance was being raised, so that Blanford came, in his spare time, to be one of the team of people helping Stewart to prepare for the eventuality of Fairfields being saved.

Another "seconded" member of this team was Bill Hawkins, who was collected into Stewart's net at Thomson House. During one of the earliest meetings there Stewart referred to the bad press he was getting and complained of how the newspapermen were trailing him and constantly misinterpreting. "What should I do?" asked Stewart.

"You need someone like Bill Hawkins," answered Harry Henry, one of the Thomson Directors, pointing to Thomson's public relations manager sitting with them. That was the last Thomson saw of his man. Stewart took Bill back up to Glasgow with him that same evening, used the plane journey to explain the whole project and established Hawkins as one of the organisation working behind the scenes to prepare for the takeover.

It happened, therefore, that on the night of 21 December Bill Hawkins was manning the telephone in Stewart's Thermotank office, whilst Oliver Blanford was standing by the only other available night line. They acted as a communications centre, in touch with the DEA in London (also working overtime), George Brown's flat, Iain Stewart's various abodes in London and Glasgow and the home addresses of a number of private and wealthy businessmen who might be able to make a decision about investment in time to salvage the project. One of these was Hugh Stenhouse.

Hugh Stenhouse is head of a mighty insurance group and

wields a mighty personality to make things go the way he wants them. He can pound the best boardroom tables with a powerful fist and still maintain a smile in his eyes to show he is enjoying the moment. No one is more forthright in his views.

The moment that the plans for Fairfields had become known he had warmed to the idea of something constructive being done for Clyde shipbuilding. He had been at prep school with Iain Stewart. Hugh Stenhouse is a great believer in leadership and he saw that Stewart could be the leader that the Fairfields yard, and then other branches of industry might follow. It was an opportunity to be grasped with both hands and he was dismayed to see so little support forthcoming from Scotland's own businessmen. When it was suggested that he might wish to support the experiment he readily offered £25 000. His business friends laughed and called him a "bloody idiot."

"Scots," explains Stenhouse, "are brave people who will risk anything except cash."

In those early days, Iain Stewart accepted Stenhouse's offer of £25 000 and promised to cover that with perhaps £25 000 of his own money if it seemed right later on. However, during the days that followed it was decided by Palmar and Stewart that it would be better to divorce the promotion of the project entirely from the financial investment, so Stewart had to be free from any suggestion of personal profit which might be made by the men, the unions or competitive shipbuilders. At the last moment, therefore, when there was still a gap to be filled in the capital backing, Hugh Stenhouse was again approached and asked if he would be willing to double his stake to fill the £50 000 slot. He agreed.

On the night of 21 December, officials at the Board of Trade were fitting together all the pieces of the Fairfield jigsaw to see if they added up to the picture of a viable new enterprise. They found one piece missing—Stenhouse.

A series of panic calls set Hawkins and Blanford hot on the trail of the one missing investor and they tracked him down, late in the evening, to his last place of call in London just before he was to take the sleeper train back up to Scotland. Blanford held Stenhouse on one phone whilst Hawkins held the Board of Trade on the other, to complete the communications circuit. Stenhouse was persuaded to dash into a cab and rush off to the Board of Trade in London on his way to Euston Station. There he found a bleary-eyed set of officials holding out a document and a pen. Hugh Stenhouse did not like the terms for "A" and "B" shareholders and he "kicked up hell" on the spot. He refused to sign. Iain Stewart could not be traced quickly enough. (He had had another fierce row with George Brown and was drowning his sorrows with friends.) Derek Palmar was located in Glasgow and he was able to authorise some of the changes demanded by Stenhouse. Agreement was reached on some amendments and, with great reluctance, but in order to avoid disaster, Stenhouse put his name to a commitment of £50 000 for shares in the new Fairfields. The 3000 jobs at the yard were saved.

On the afternoon of Wednesday 22 December 1965, George Brown could at last stand up in the House of Commons and make an historic reply to John Rankin's simple question:

> Would my Right Honourable Friend care to make a statement about the future of the Fairfield ship-building company?

The First Secretary of State was able to answer:

> Although I am not yet in a position to give the House the details, I am glad to be able to say that arrangements have been made to safeguard the future of Fairfields shipyard. This will reassure not

only the people working in the yard, but also the
shipowners who, from a sense of patriotism and
generosity, have kept orders with the yard and sub-
contractors who have continued to supply equipment to the yard despite the uncertainty which
has clouded its future.

I am glad to say that we now have the founda-
tion for a financial partnership between the
Government, private enterprise and the Trade
Unions as a result of which this shipyard can continue. The private enterprise partners will consist
of Mr Iain Stewart [Iain Stewart never held shares.
This was an "umbrella" remark, covering the unnamed associates Stenhouse and Salvesen.] and his
associates; Lord Thomson of Fleet; Sir Isaac
Wolfson; and others with whom we are currently
discussing the position. In addition two of our
major Trade Unions have expressed their intention
of participating, and discussions are going on with
others.

The Government will hold half of the equity
of the new company Fairfield (Glasgow) Limited.
The other half will be shared between the other
partners. This will enable the shipyard to operate
as a commercial concern. The shipyard will need,
in addition to the equity, loan capital and this the
Government is prepared to provide on normal
terms. These arrangements do not extend to the
engineering works Fairfield-Rowan Limited.

The Chairman of the new company will be Mr
Iain Stewart, whose wide business interests are
already closely associated with the West of Scotland, and Govan in particular.

In backing this new concept in British business
all the partners, the Government, private enterprise and the Trade Unions are relying on the men

in the yard to co-operate unreservedly in working the yard as efficiently as possible and in particular in achieving the flexible manning arrangements and interchangeability of workers which are essential. If this co-operation were not forthcoming the whole scheme involving the combined support of Government, the Unions and private enterprise would fall to the ground and the shipyard would have to close.

I am sure the House will welcome our action as a quite new partnership not only between Government and private enterprise, but now between Government, private enterprise and the Trade Unions; the motive being not merely to save a recently modernised Scottish shipyard from extinction, important as that would be, but, in addition, to provide a proving-ground for new relations in the shipbuilding industry which could change the whole image of our country.

Brown was effervescent at the successful climax to the days of slog and argument. Immediately after the announcement in the House he bounced across the courtyard outside and shouted to one of his junior ministers, Edmund Dell, "I've just bought you a shipyard."

When the four Fairfield shop stewards arrived back in Glasgow the banners were flying.

WE'VE WON!
MERRY CHRISTMAS AFTER ALL!
YOUR TRIP WAS NOT IN VAIN!

There was a mass reception of 5000 men giving the thumbs-up sign, chanting Merry Christmas, singing, laughing and whooping with delight.

The banner headlines were also flying in the newspapers. "Fairfields safe," "Boy with a future," "Exciting partnership," "New image for industry," "Union-Bosses link salvages shipyard" were the shouts from every shade of the press.

The Times ended its leader with the words: "Mr Brown is taking a reasonable risk. Mr Stewart is being given an opportunity to prove his ideas. The unions are on trial. What is at stake is the future of Britain's shipyards. Fairfield could be the spur that the yards have needed for so long."

Immediately the muzzle was taken off Iain Stewart and he could speak to the men. A mass meeting was planned for Monday 27 December, in the Lyceum Cinema near the yard. Stewart was determined, still, not to go ahead with the project without a definite reliable "pledge" from the men of complete co-operation in his plans.

At eight o'clock on Monday morning, after a "bonanza" Christmas weekend in Govan, 3000 men crowded into the cinema for their first taste of direct communication with their new boss. Iain Stewart is disparagingly referred to in some Glasgow circles as a "tub-thumper." His enemies like to think that he can sway men to follow him purely through demagogic appeal. In fact he is a poor speaker for mass audiences, a nervous speaker who does not feel at ease when faced with the task of communicating difficult ideas to a large assembly. He is far more persuasive when debating with a small gathering in a lounge or cocktail bar or when making his points on a telephone. He was now obliged to stand in the vast Lyceum cinema at eight o'clock on a winter's morning and convince 3000 shipyard workers that they should forget their union rule books and negotiate future employment conditions purely on the basis of what was best for productivity. He also had to ask them to agree to isolate Fairfields from all contracts negotiated by their mates in other firms, so that their yard would not be fettered by any national, district or local agreements.

They would have to promise to eliminate strikes, go-slows and overtime bans. Most important of all, the men must be willing to allow free movement between jobs as demand fluctuated and to co-operate in all the modern management techniques of job evaluation and work study to ensure that ships could be delivered on time and at a profit.

(Iain Stewart was in no way sure of the reply he would get. There is still in existence a statement he prepared for the press to use at any convenient time to express his disappointment that his plans had not been successful. This opens with the words:

> I am bitterly disappointed that the Fairfield project has fallen through and I feel it necessary to place on record a review of my own participation in this project. . . . I am hopeful that the recent events will bring nearer the day when industry will accept those principles of employment for which I have been fighting for many years. The introduction of these conditions will not be easy and will demand great understanding and endless patience. I am only sorry that it has not been possible to come to grips with the deeply rooted problems of the craft industries.)

Stewart spoke to the men at the Lyceum mass meeting at great length, reading eleven pages of typewritten script. It was coolly delivered, his theme closely argued line by line without appeal to easy emotionalism. In return for the sacrifices he demanded, he offered re-training to eliminate the fear of unemployment, union representation on the Board of Fairfields and regular reports direct from him to the men on how things were going.

Stewart stated that he was prepared to accept their public endorsement of his conditions. "There need be no agreement in writing—it will simply be based on mutual trust for if we are not prepared to trust you—then we can hardly expect you to trust us."

THE MILLIONAIRES' ROUND-UP

He ended his speech with: "Mr George Brown calls me
with some affection I think 'that bloody Tory,' on the other
hand some of my Tory colleagues—also with some affection
I hope—call me 'that bloody Communist.' ... In my book,
as an industrialist, efficient industry must be run the same
way regardless of which Government is in power.

"Gentlemen, do you accept these conditions of employment or do you not?"

The men applauded his words and, with roars of "We're
with you Iain!" voted by a show of hands to follow him all
the way. This pledge went very deep and the men regarded it
as a solemn oath they had sworn. Although there was no
written agreement, the television newsreels had evidence
enough what they had voted for. It was the beginning of the
"discipline of publicity" which Stewart introduced into the
yard. Every move made by the men and the management
became a national talking point, discussed in radio and TV
programmes, argued out in the press, described in features
and interviews. The yard became a "goldfish bowl," with
all the fish, big fish and little fish, under such close scrutiny
that there could be no backsliding without a public outcry.
After all, the public had its own money invested through
the Board of Trade which became the holder of the Government shares.

The Observer, the following Sunday, commented, "What
it adds up to is an unprecedented new deal in labour-
management agreement which could, just possibly, set the
pattern for a revolution in industrial relations throughout
the country."

In the *Sunday Mirror* Alex Jamieson was reported as
saying: "Till now shipyard workers have shown their
muscles to the bosses because it was necessary. But under
this revolutionary set-up outlined by Mr Stewart this will become a thing of the past. When I heard he had been
appointed I rang him up from home on a Sunday morning
at ten o'clock. My wife, Jennie, told me that I had a hell of

a cheek. But Mr Stewart talked to me for a full half hour. He put his position on the line, fairly and bluntly in a friendly fashion. This was in confidence, before he spoke to us all at a mass meeting. My estimation of him went right up."

But Stewart's administration was not allowed the usual 100 days honeymoon. Before the new company, Fairfields (Glasgow) Limited, was actually formed on 7 January the worst crisis to date hit the project, taking Stewart and Brown to the lowest depths of depression they had reached during the whole campaign.

The major unions which had promised to invest, the AEU, Brown's own union the TGWU, and the General and Municipal Workers Union, suddenly withdrew.

It had been discovered that their constitutions did not allow them to invest their funds in any enterprise which carried an undue risk. No one could claim that shares in Fairfields would be gilt-edged securities.

As soon as the unions stepped down, Roy Thomson also cried off, for his entry had been prompted by the idea of complete union participation and integration. Isaac Wolfson followed Thomson out, leaving only Salvesen and Stenhouse's £150 000 out of the required £530 000.

When this news came through to Stewart, George Brown was quietly relaxing at a friend's house in Scotland, convalescing from the strains of the previous two months. Brown had once already interrupted his holiday to visit the Fairfield yard and Fairfield-Rowan engineering works in Govan, where he had made a big hit addressing the assembled workforce. Just when there seemed no more clouds on the Fairfield front, this new storm burst.

Iain Stewart raced up to see the Minister and, in company with some other advisers, they tried to thrash out a solution. But there seemed no way out. Fairfields was once again doomed. The effect of such an announcement would obviously cause great damage to the Government's prestige, especially after all the junketing when the crisis had been thought resolved at last. George Brown had staked his political reputation on success and so, he argued, he would have to take the consequences.

The arguments and the recriminations against investors, unions, Government, life in general went on and on over dinner and wine. At one point George Brown thumped so hard to emphasise his point that he hit his soup plate and had a lapful of scotch broth to add to his troubles.

At last, when there seemed total deadlock without a straw left to grasp at, George Brown went to the telephone and sent a message to the Prime Minister. He was offering his resignation.

In the depressed lull that followed, Iain Stewart suddenly saw a solution. He could keep Thomson and Wolfson in by underwriting their investment. He would guarantee their cash personally against the eventuality of the unions' not being able to participate. If the unions were not able to take up shares, then Stewart would purchase Thomson's and Wolfson's shares.

It was an enormous risk that Stewart would be undertaking, because it would mean that he would only own shares if things went wrong and would not be a shareholder if things went right. He had everything to lose and nothing to gain financially.

Furthermore it should be seen in the context of his other business activities, his battle to save his own firm and his own fortune at Hall-Thermotank.

George Brown knew his background and interpreted Stewart's gesture as a personal sacrifice to save Brown's career. He would not accept Stewart's proposal.

"You are just trying to save my political future," Brown wailed.

"I don't give a damn for your politics," shouted Stewart, "only for the principles behind Fairfields."

Derek Palmar was one of the advisers present. He saw

that if Iain Stewart was willing to take that step it was a way out of disaster. It might at the very least provide a breathing space, with always the chance to replace Thomson and Wolfson with other investors if only time were made available. The new company was due to be officially formed the next morning, so that it could purchase the assets from the Fairfield Receiver. If there were another delay, then the shipowners who had ships and orders with the Fairfield yard would be obliged to take them away to other yards, foreign yards probably. Fairfields would be finished for ever and all their efforts totally wasted and many reputations ruined. It would be a worse blow for the Clyde, for Scotland and the DEA Regional Policy than if the yard had been allowed to close in the first place, without the hullaballoo.

There was also a member of the Council of the Glasgow Corporation present who could reinforce the view that what Stewart was offering was in Glasgow's and the nation's interest, not just for the sake of Brown's political future.

At last George Brown agreed to fall in with Stewart's plan. A statement was typed out on a handy bit of plain paper. Derek Palmar cast his City eye over this and made alterations in handwriting, stipulating specific sums of money in place of a more vague phraseology. The final undertaking read thus:

> Although certain major Trades Unions have publicly stated their intention to invest in Fairfields (Glasgow) Limited; and the First Secretary of State has announced this in the House of Commons: doubts have been expressed in the Press whether these Trades Unions will in the event be in a position to honour their undertakings.
>
> The existing private enterprise partners feel that, should this unlikely event occur, it might well create a new situation. They (or some of them)

might then wish to relinquish their holdings in the enterprise at the end of six months.

In that event, other private enterprise interests, represented by Mr Iain Stewart, will undertake to arrange for these interests to be taken over at a price to be agreed between the parties.

It should be re-emphasised that this undertaking relates only to the possibility that the Trades Unions will not honour their undertaking to participate financially in the equity of the company to the extent of at least £100 000.

I agree to the foregoing.

George Brown   Iain Stewart   6 January 1966

It took six months for the unions to go through the democratic procedure of amending their constitutions or finding other means to permit them to invest some risk capital in Fairfields. The Electrical Trades Union, for example, never took shares, but instead provided £50 000 as a loan with 5 per cent interest, thus sidestepping the restriction in their rules. The press and the public thought the unions' inability to invest, when announced, was a point-blank refusal to become involved and heralded the end of the Fairfields idea, but the document signed by Brown and Stewart kept up their spirits whilst lengthy negotiations went on with the unions behind the scenes. Meanwhile, the new Fairfields company could take over the yard and start operating. The union cash, finally adding up to £180 000, was not immediately vital. The Government and private investments were sufficient to purchase the assets required and Government loans were available for working capital.

When the two signatures had been appended to the strange document, George Brown then cancelled his resignation and Iain Stewart was at last able to turn his mind to the real problem of transforming a bankrupt shipyard into a profitable enterprise. It was hard to recall that the main aim of

E

all that behind-the-scenes activity was the construction of ships at a competitive yet profitable price and their delivery to owners on time.

In his first letter to Brown, forty-eight days previously, Stewart had promised "to produce a profit on the Fairfield balance sheet, certainly within five years and probably within three." That was his next assignment.

Chapter four

What They Found at Fairfields

There was one man in the old Fairfield Drawing Office who was said to have drawn over 1000 perfect lavatory bowls in his time there. His work had probably cost the company £10 000.

Jim Houston, the man appointed to head the new management techniques department of Fairfields (Glasgow) Limited as the Productivity Services Director, sent a three-man productivity team into the drawing office originally out of simple curiosity. It had been an accepted thing in more sophisticated industries that the draughtsmen's work was one of the most difficult to organise for increased productivity and it had not been listed as a priority task when Stewart's new management took over.

Houston, a pugnacious Glaswegian from lowly beginnings but with a lofty future, had been grabbed from Singer Sewing Machines by Oliver Blanford. A management consultant friend of Blanford had heard that a top man was being sought to head the productivity crusade in Fairfield and he told him: "If you are looking for a really dynamic bastard, I can point him out." It was Houston, forty-three-year-old Director of Engineering at Singer's in Clydebank, a fearless, total convert to productivity, who was beginning to scare the pants off the olde-worlde employers in the district. Stewart could see what Fairfields would be in for when they met for a final interview. They had arranged to meet at nine-thirty for dinner at the Malmaison in Glasgow. At seven-thirty Stewart already had a dinner engagement at the same place, but he did not want to postpone seeing Houston, as he was so urgently in need of senior executives for Fairfields. Stewart had aperitifs, dinner and brandies with his first dinner guest (a Director of Scottish Television), made his farewells and then darted to the Malmaison bar to be there to greet Houston. They began on the gin and tonics and whiskys then went in for dinner. The waiter was the same one who had just served Stewart, so he only set cutlery for Houston. The first question Houston asked his future Chairman was: "Don't you use eating irons?" Stewart did not want Houston to know what lengths he had gone to in order to be able to talk over dinner with him. He went through the motion of eating a second dinner.

Houston had been approached to join Fairfields but had expressed many doubts. He did not personally think there was much hope for British shipbuilding in the face of foreign competition and he was not convinced that a British shipbuilding company would accept the tremendous changes necessary in order to fight this competition. The dinner with Stewart removed these doubts, until there was only one point which upset him. He looked at the rather clinical job specification which Blanford had drawn up for the Productivity Services Director.

"I've got a set of rules here," he said, "which say that I shall be expected to commence work at 7 45 a.m. and finish at 5 p.m. I'm not in the habit of being told when to start and when to stop work. In any case, I'm certain we'll need to work more hours than that if we are to accomplish this task. It's the challenge that counts."

Stewart crossed out the offending clause and Houston joined Fairfields, to work an average of over eighty hours a week for two years, setting the pattern for the rest of his staff. He was able to bring into Fairfields over the next few months a highly talented group of young managers specialised in productivity techniques and training.

When his appointment was announced to the Fairfield men, along with so many other newcomers who had had no experience whatsoever in the shipbuilding industry, there was some feeling of alarm amongst the workers.

"Bloody hell," they complained in the pubs, "from Singer's! We'll soon be sewing the ships plates together, not welding 'em." They had to avoid clubs and pubs where there was a danger of meeting mates from other yards, for the Fairfields men became the butt of widespread ridicule. Literally scores of men were soon issuing from Houston's department armed with stop watches, tape measures and notebooks. Safety helmets were issued, colour coded to indicate the nature of a person's employment. "God," the yard workers exclaimed, "a bunch of bloody chocolate Smarties!"

Houston and his merry men were aghast at what was uncovered in the yard. The drawing office exploratory foraging proved to be amazingly fruitful, for example. For a century that department had prided itself on its standard of work. When producing the drawings for the New Zealand ferry *Wahine*, the draughtsman had painted in the most magnificent colour representation of the New Zealand flag flying from the stern. "Hang the painting in the Royal Academy," ordered Houston, "and the draughtsman from the yardarm of the ship!" He was convinced that the only reason for putting in the flag was to enable people to tell the back end of the ship from the front, a problem which never failed to cause him difficulty, especially as modern merchant ships have bulbous bows.

It was discovered that in the drawing office no attention had been paid to reducing the time spent on drawings. Instead of being regarded purely and simply as a means of a designer telling an engineer what has to be constructed, the drawings were looked upon as typifying the quality of the finished product. So, in one instance, a draughtsman had painstakingly drawn all 740 little stools in the ship's cocktail bar. Each of the ship's lifeboats was a separately depicted work of art.

At one point the productivity team in the drawing office could not concentrate on their work because of the rhythmic thumping noise coming from the neighbouring office. When they looked in they found one of the draughtsmen, almost hidden by the stacks of drawings around him, intensely occupied in stamping each one with a huge rubber stamp. He was imprinting the legend: THIS DRAWING NOT REQUIRED.

As Houston says, everyone was working hard and doing things right, but they were just not doing the right things. On one occasion, when a department asked permission to employ extra labour for manual work, Houston dragged the department head with him on a tour of the yard. "You can have the first man we find doing something not worthwhile," he promised. They entered the nearest fabrication shop, an enormous building holding hundreds of men and machines. There they came across workmen whose job it was to sweep the shop, armed with a tiny midget of a brush "suffering badly from dandruff and falling hair." Later the arrangement was made for each machine operator to give his own immediate area a quick brush around as relaxation from a repetitive job. This could only be achieved when "interchangeability" and "flexibility" had been fully approved.

Oliver Blanford recounts some of the wasteful activities which cried out for change when he took over as General Manager of Fairfields (Glasgow) Limited.

My findings during my first three months at Fairfields were that they made good quality ships, though by no means as good as they thought, and not always at the first or even fourth attempt. There

60

was little technology outside a small group in the drawing office.

Time-keeping amongst the men was thoroughly bad, about 15 per cent being more than a quarter of an hour late every day and absenteeism shocking at around 17 per cent.

We sold some £25 000 worth of redundant stores. Some of the items dated back to the late 1890s and quite a few to the 1914–18 War.

We found that in most weeks around 8 per cent of items being delivered to the company from outside suppliers were rejects and had to be returned or rectified. In some weeks and from some suppliers the reject rate went up to as high as 40 per cent.

Previously these items were built into ships and found to be defective on test, when they had to be removed or rectified on site.

This was in Britain's "most modern yard"! It seemed typical of the attitude in other yards. Two years later, Fairfields (Glasgow) Limited entered negotiations for a possible merger with the John Brown yard at Clydebank, the yard which built the QE2. A report of the discussions quotes John Rannie, then Managing Director of John Brown (Clydebank), as arguing that with the Cunarder (QE2) on his hands he could not risk the upset and interference which would be involved in the introduction of work study.

"Anyway," he is quoted as saying, "where could I get the staff?"

Rannie maintained then he could not at that stage advise his Board to use methods different from those in use on the Q4 (as the ship was called before the launching). On quality control, Rannie argued that the high quality of John Brown's labour at Clydebank was the best guarantee of quality and they had no formal machinery for quality control.

He claimed there were no rejections on grounds of inadequate quality of work from the pipeshop at Clydebank. He is quoted as saying:

"We could not afford an inspector. The first test is when the pipes are assembled and oil and water is pumped through."

That discussion was reported on 11 October 1966, more than two years before the QE2 had to cut short its trials because of faults in its oil and water system, with oil leaking into the boiler tubes.

"Ah," people sympathised from other industries, "when you think of all the quality control tests that valve system must have been through, damn bad luck to have a failure on the trials."

The QE2 affair also brought the spotlight on to the pilfering which went on in Clyde yards. This was nothing new. The new management at Fairfields marvelled at the expertise shown by the thieves. They discovered that there were high walls around the yard and sturdy gates with experienced gatemen on duty, but no defence whatsoever against boats being rowed up the river at night, tied up alongside the slipways on the waterfront and loaded with vast quantities of materials. Fairfields put a watch on the waterfront and managed to reduce the theft of cable, for example, from around £150 a week (with a measured peak in the early days of £270 a week) down to about £25 a week. Previously no proper system of stock control had operated so that no one knew what, if anything, was being stolen.

A few months after the introduction of the stricter security measures a number of the formerly prosperous second-hand and scrap dealers in Govan closed down.

The new men expected to be able to teach new techniques and methods to Fairfields, but they also expected that they would find that the workers knew their trades. In many instances this was not so. Once documentation had been initiated to keep track of what progress was being achieved at every stage in the building of a ship, distinguishing between good work and abortive work, they were horrified at some of the poor quality that came to light. It was true that Clyde-built ships were of the finest quality once handed over to their owners, but the great problem was the amount of work which had to be done several times over before it was right. One plate for the hull of a naval ship was installed and taken out again eight times. The men on the job were paid for all the time they spent, but the yard was only being paid by the Navy for putting the plate in once.

The Quality Control teams delved into this and found that the problem was the poor quality of the welding which was repeatedly distorting the plate in situ. They demanded a retesting of the skills of all the welders. Due to the already improved relations created between unions and management, these tests were agreed. They uncovered the unsavoury fact that over 60 per cent of the yard's welders (very highly paid "skilled" men) failed to reach the minimum standards of proficiency. They were not downgraded, but immediately retrained. They had the innate ability to reach the highest standards but they had been neglected and left to pick up skills as best they could with totally inadequate instruction.

The biggest and most troublesome union (from the Clyde shipbuilders' point of view) had always been the Boilermakers, or, to give the union its full name, The Amalgamated Society of Boilermakers, Shipwrights, Blacksmiths and Structural Workers. They prided themselves on being tough nuts who would not easily succumb to "brainwashing" by the bosses. Pat Kelly, who was then the local delegate for the Boilermakers, has since remarked; "The new management said they didn't know how to build ships, but they certainly showed us how to. The men knew they had a good management, they appreciated it and therefore they co-operated."

When the men were posed simple questions about methods of work, they constantly gave the answer that things were done that way because they had always been done that way and they had always worked. Nobody seemed to notice that they had, in fact, stopped working, for Britain, the proud shipbuilding country, had now fallen right out of the race for world orders, with output actually falling whilst world tonnage launched was increasing rapidly. Our industry was shrinking whilst that of our main competitors was expanding.

One of the simple straightforward questions was: "Why do you start building a ship from the pointed end?" "We always have," was the reply. It had never been considered in any other way. All ships on the Clyde had always been begun at the bow and constructed gradually down towards the stern. "Ah," explained the new men from other industries, "but if you started from the stern, then whilst you were putting the rest of the hull together all the other trades could be busy installing the main engines and the auxilliary equipment and fitting out the cabins for the crew." In tankers and bulk carriers, the ships engines and living quarters are now usually located aft, leaving the rest of the hull free to serve as a giant container for the cargo.

From then onwards Fairfield ships were constructed from the stern, working forwards. However, the new management's pride at this innovation received a jolt when their investigations later uncovered the fact that the Japanese were starting in the middle of their ships, with two teams of men able to work forwards and rearwards simultaneously, getting the ship off the stocks in less than half the time and gaining world orders by guaranteeing quicker delivery dates.

As the first months went by, more and more facts were assembled by the 130 work study specialists put to work by Blanford and Houston. The information was gleaned which would make it possible to put right things which had obviously been very wrong but which, previously, nobody was able to pinpoint. Information was vital to the new bosses, for they could make no definite moves forward until they had decided what needed doing and in what priority.

It was found, for example, that the average working week per man was thirty-seven and a half hours. That, believe it or not, included two nights of overtime and a double-pay Sunday! Men were in the habit of going absent and turning up late during the week and then making up their wage packet with the more lucrative overtime rates. Their working habits had to be changed, and, maintains Houston, there also have to be changes in social habits, for in Japan the shipyards have three shifts, in Sweden two shifts whilst in Britain they do one shift. Again, this means that capital equipment is used for only a small proportion of the day and delivery dates are lengthened beyond the limits set by the customers, the shipowners. Once a shipping company decides it needs a new ship it is usually keen to get it as soon as it can.

When the Geddes Report was published in March 1966 it confirmed that most of the disastrous facts about Fairfield were common to the majority of UK yards. It took eighty-seven manhours for UK shipyards to build an equivalent ton of steel whereas the figure for Japan was twenty-nine hours. The Japanese, through improved techniques, better layout of yards and a greater amount of modern equipment, were able to produce ships with only one third of the effort. This comparison already allowed for the differences in type of work, so there was no excuse that they built mainly tankers requiring simple steelwork, whilst UK concentrated on the more complex merchant ships.

The Clyde statistics showed an average of 110 manhours per equivalent ton of steel! This was almost four times less economic than Japanese competition.

Management and men were to blame for the poor state of the yards. During the boom time of 1945 to 1950 British yards could sell everything they could make. Our yards were intact at the end of the war, whilst most of the competitive ones were in ruins. There was a surging demand for new ships to replace the merchant fleets sunk during hostilities. Owners got in the queue for ships and were happy to take delivery whenever the ship was ready and to pay a price which consisted of costs plus a profit to the yard. (Not far removed from the present system of building ships for the Admiralty.) It was virtually impossible for the yards to go wrong. Big profits were made, but shipyard facilities hardly benefited from this cash. Insufficient investment was made in new equipment; an absence of research meant that the giant tankers of the future were not foreseen and no berths were laid down to cater for them; the industry was so inward looking and self-satisfied that the striking new developments taking place in the reconstruction of German and Japanese yards were not clearly appreciated. Sweden, too, went ahead with developments, even though its yards had not been destroyed by war. Sweden made a detailed survey of shipbuilding and, like the Japanese, decided it was just another form of industrial manufacture. So new yards were built which operated like factories. Parts of the hull were prefabricated and lifted and welded into position inside a factory, under cover. As the ship grew in length, so it was gradually eased bit by bit out of a giant opening, with the end under construction still under cover.

The unions and men in British shipbuilding also contributed towards its stagnation. "You don't negotiate, you stand up and fight like men," is one typical comment, which was made by a Clyde shop steward in a family-owned yard. The jobs and the methods of work should have been changed but unions hung on to old practices. The unemployment of the 'thirties was still a solid, real memory in all the shipyard workers' homes. There was a continuous civil war, in almost feudal conditions, at most yards, to an extent that is unbelievable to people who did not personally witness it.

Oliver Blanford remembers how he was first shown to a gathering of the Scottish TUC on Saturday 31 December

1965. It was Hogmanay and George Brown was to address them about his hopes for their co-operation in the new Fairfields venture. Oliver Blanford, not yet officially on the staff of the new company, was introduced by Brown as the new General Manager. After his short speech, Blanford was approached by a Trade Union official who asked if he would do one particular favour when the yard got going.

"Certainly," said Blanford, "what is it?"

"Do you think you could arrange more comfortable conditions for us to meet our members in the yard?"

"Well," asked Blanford, "what actually happens now?"

"Oh," the old trade unionist explained, "we're not allowed in to see them and they're not allowed out to see us, otherwise it's called a wildcat strike, so we stand and discuss our matters through the iron bars in the main gate. The trouble is, you see, it so often is raining."

Blanford kept his promise and one of the first tasks of the new management at Fairfields was to construct a conference room where shop stewards could hold their meetings. When asked recently what were the main achievements at Fairfields, Pat Kelly, the hard-headed Boilermakers warrior who had been a shop steward himself for twelve years, placed that conference room top of the list. It was an invaluable investment.

On the same day, Hogmanay 1965, Blanford made another promise. It was in reply to a specific instruction from George Brown. "Oliver," Brown said to him, "do one thing for me when you get inside that yard. Get rid of the bowlers."

Bowler hats were the sign of management status and they cut the men off from management like an electrified fence. On principle none of the new intake wore a bowler. Instead they went round the yard, usually, with safety helmets, a sign of the new efficiency era. They wanted the men to wear safety helmets, too, but this never caught on. If any of the old managers in the yard tried to hold on to their bowler, they were just laughed at by the others. "Why on earth are you wearing that ridiculous thing?" they were constantly asked until they just gave them up.

So much a symbol of the "boss class" were bowlers, that Sean Connery, when he made a film of Fairfields later, called the film *The Bowler and the Bunnet*, the bunnet being the little cloth cap worn by the shipyard workers. His film showed how the old gulf between management and men could be crossed by the new approach introduced by Iain Stewart. Sean Connery had met Stewart accidentally at a London golf club dinner. When he heard in more detail of the experiment being carried out at Fairfields he felt all the old resentment against management being reawakened inside himself. Connery had held eight different union cards in his early days as milkman and labourer and factory worker. He recalled all the disenchantment and also all the feelings of revenge which had been predominant in the workforce of which he had been a part, in Scotland.

He accepted an invitation to visit the yard and, once there, he determined to make a film of what was going on. "To me," he explains, "it sounded like the definite solution to Britain's malaise." He gave six weeks of his time free of charge to make *The Bowler and the Bunnet* for Scottish Television and it was also subsequently shown at private screenings for Tory and Labour gatherings in London (separate occasions, of course). On the first occasion, the *Bowler and the Bunnet* was followed by a newly made film of the Upper Clyde merger. This introduced the managers of the other yards—all wearing bowlers.

The men in the Clyde yards never said "good morning" or anything to the bosses when they passed but looked resolutely ahead as if they had not seen them. As recounted in an earlier chapter, The Govan MP, John Rankin, was not allowed in any of the yards except in the last couple of years at the old Fairfields after a chance meeting with a director, and, once in Fairfields, his bowler-hatted escort would never join in any chats with the workers.

The new management was disgusted at the wretched conditions in the toilets and in the men's canteen which was Dickensian in its drab, dingy, workhouse-like atmosphere, with negligible light, barrack-room tables and cold stone floors. Two new canteens were another priority investment. Neither did the men have any kind of cloakroom or lockers to hang up their coats and jackets. It had always been the custom to leave these lying around on the floor wherever they were working, amongst the oil, grease, steel scraps and filings. At the tea breaks everyone had to troop over to the canteen from wherever they were employed, so that those in the bowels of the ships had to climb up on deck, over the side of the hull and walk across the sprawling yard, a journey which wasted many working hours during a week.

The directors' working conditions were a world apart. The main mahogany-panelled Boardroom, formerly used about once every three months, was converted by Stewart into a general dining room and used every day by staff and guests, including trade unionists. On the occasion of the first launching of the *British Commodore* described at the opening of the book, this room accommodated the whole reception for the 250 guests and officials.

It was this kind of action taken by Stewart which convinced many of the other local industrialists that he was definitely a "red." One story relates how he was playing golf with Michael Medwin, the actor and film producer. Stewart tee'd off with a mighty swipe and then lost sight of the flight of the ball. "Which way did it go?" he asked Medwin. Suddenly, from behind a hedge, a very aristocratic Scottish voice called out: "Straight down the left, like your bloody politics!"

In addition to all these failings, there was one major and fundamental fault in the shipbuilding system which was a root cause of the head-on collison between men and management. A big proportion of the labour force on the Clyde, and in the other shipbuilding centres of Britain, was "nomadic."

As one shop steward explains: "Every time a new ship hit the water a batch of men would be paid off. So, a few weeks before, if another yard was busy on a new order, half the lads would bugger off to get in there first and be sure of a few months more work. If there weren't any other ships coming along on the Clyde, then they'd say 'Well, let's get what we can out of this one.' The way they looked at it, it was in their interests to keep the ship delayed and keep themselves in work."

In either case a ship nearing completion was held back, because the men stretched the work out or because there were not enough men, suddenly, to finish the job. The QE2 suffered badly through this before its launching as it was the only ship John Brown's had in their yard of any size and its launch was scheduled for not long before Christmas. Who wants to work hard to put himself on the dole for Christmas?

Because of a dire lack of training or personnel control, departmental heads could scream for extra men and get them whenever they felt in a panic. "Twenty hands needed right away in the steelwork section!" was the call and twenty men were duly hired. In a couple of weeks time the work could have run out, or it might not even have materialised for them to do. Then those men were paid off and were back on the streets looking for work.

There were also complex systems of pay differentials, so that as many as 500 rates of pay were running concurrently in one company. So jealously did the men guard their differentials and guard the available work, that a main theme of union activity was a fight against changes—against changes in rate structures, against the loss of work to another type of tradesman, against the loss of an exclusive right to a certain type of job.

Stewart stressed from the very beginning of his cam-

paign that fear was the basis of the men-management confrontation, fear based on insecurity. Unemployment was a
constant threat to their lives, to the welfare of their
families.

"Unemployment soon means premature retirement," they
explain. "We had the highest unemployment rate in the
country. When a man has no work he rots away and becomes a forgotten man."

It was easy for an outsider, like Stewart, to see that the
delays to the delivery of ships, the increased prices due to
overmanning and the waste of materials and time, the failure
to invest in new ideas and equipment, all meant certain
ruin for the men and the management in British shipbuilding. But the cycle of action and reaction, resentment and
revenge was one which could only be interrupted by decisive
blows. That was why he had suggested in his letter to
Brown that "psychologically the worse things are, the easier
it will be to solve the problem." And things were certainly
bad at Fairfields on the Clyde.

Jealousy over jobs meant strict demarcation not only between unions but also between trades inside the same union.
"One man one job" had been the slogan for 150 years and
it applied, for example, to the ten or more distinct trades
inside the Boilermakers Society, so that a shipwright could
not drill a hole, a blacksmith was not allowed to weld.
There were caulkers, platers, shipwrights, welders, holders-
on and sheetiron workers, all with strict limitations on what
they were permitted to do. One worker explained how it
took three men all afternoon to fix an electric cable on the
ship's bulkhead. The electrician would go and find his own
foreman and ask for a driller. His foreman would contact
the foreman of the drillers and ask for a man to be sent.
When a driller had been spared and had drilled a couple of
holes, the electrician would then ask his foreman to locate
a caulker to prepare the holes for his fixtures. The same
procedure was repeated and then at last, after the various

breaks and delays, the electrician was allowed to instal his cable.

Workers from the yards have described how, due to lack of proper control and supervision, one batch of men would spend a day fitting cabins with Formica walls and ceilings. Later, along would come the electricians to lay the cables behind the walls. The Formica would have to be ripped out and then put back again the following day, doubling the cost of the work.

The same waste through lack of planning and control went right through a whole yard's hierarchy. Brought up on the cost plus profits basis of selling ships to eager buyers, "any owner," Oliver Blanford has remarked, "any owner, but particularly the Admiralty, was granted any change, however unreasonable or costly." This compliant attitude remained the same even when ships were being built to a very keen, rigid price. The wording of contracts still offered every part of the ship "to owner's satisfaction," but now there was no way of increasing the price to cover the cost of any extra work demanded by the owner.

This chapter has been phrased mainly in the past tense. It has referred to what the new management found when they bought the yard and its assets from the Receiver of Fairfield Shipbuilding and Engineering Company Limited. It is as well to bear in mind, however, that the period under discussion was only the early months of 1966, not so long ago. These conditions apply still, not only in many shipyards, but also in many other branches of industry. Iain Stewart clung firmly to the words of George Brown's statement in the House announcing the start of a new partnership:

> In addition, to provide a proving ground for new relations in the shipbuilding industry which could change the whole image of our country.

In advance of the statement, Stewart had pressed the First Secretary of State to use the description "experiment," but

Brown was keen to put Fairfields forward as a viable commercial enterprise set up to build ships at a profit. He shied away from anything as risky as "experiment." It was Lord Shawcross who came up with the accommodating expression "proving ground" which satisfied both points of view. Shawcross acknowledges that George Brown, Iain Stewart and Derek Palmar may all claim to be father to the idea of Fairfields, but he claims to have been the midwife.

Stewart desperately wanted the chance to put his ideas for a revolution in industrial relations in Britain into practice. He wanted his new Fairfields to be under constant scrutiny so that its failures and successes could point the way for others to follow. At the same time, he had pledged himself to take Fairfields, with all its sticky history, and make it efficient and profitable within three to five years. In fact, it returned some profit in less than two.

Chapter five

Under New Management

One only needs to take a look at the list of people who became Directors on the Board of Fairfields (Glasgow) Limited to see that the venture was much more than the mere rescue of a bankrupt shipyard (no mean task, anyway).

"National proving ground," "experiment," "industrial laboratory" were descriptions Stewart took to heart. He certainly experimented, he certainly dedicated the venture to research and he made sure that what went on at Fairfields was open to the study and scrutiny of the rest of the country at every level.

Stewart placed men with different talents and influences on his Board with the skill of a chess master.

The Government's 50 per cent shareholding had to be represented. Derek Palmar was appointed as the Government Director. He had been friend and adviser to Stewart for many years and was one of the initiators of the Fairfield plan, so there was no outside bullying from the Government. (At least not until the end.) Although the Department of Economic Affairs, George Brown's Ministry, had been mainly involved in the setting-up negotiations, the shares were eventually held in the name of the Board of Trade, which was the Ministry responsible for shipbuilding at that time. Derek Palmar used to send reports to the Board of Trade, with copies for the personal attention of George Brown, who was kept in the picture about the welfare of his un-conventionally spawned offspring as he himself moved from one Ministry to another and finally out of the Government.

Frank Cousins, the Minister of Technology, argued that the Fairfield project should be in the care of his department, which was responsible for dragging Britain, kicking and screaming, into the age of advanced industry. So the share-holding was transferred to Mintech. Derek Palmar sent his reports to Frank Cousins, with copies to George Brown, by now the Foreign Secretary. Frank Cousins was replaced by Anthony Wedgwood Benn and took his turn as the recipient of the Government Director's reports on Fairfield's progress. Wedgwood Benn was so much an outsider to the Fairfield baby that he played more the part of disinterested stepfather than benevolent uncle. It was at that point that the Government started to bring pressure to bear. George Brown, by his resignation from the Cabinet, had by then lost any claim to the child and became a helpless onlooker.

Iain Stewart, in spite of a naïveté which makes him some-times imagine that the world can be expected to lay down its prejudices and vested interests in support of a worth-while idea, was realist enough to expect opposition from the other shipbuilders. But his optimism led him to believe that they would co-operate if he gave them every opportunity to become involved. In the early days of December, when the structure of the company was being worked out, he offered places on the new Board to a couple of the leading shipyard-owning families on the Clyde.

He wrote to Jim Stephen of Stephen's Yard and Sir Eric Yarrow of Yarrow's Yard, inviting them to serve as Direc-tors if the project got going, explaining that they would then, from a privileged position, be able to satisfy themselves that Fairfields was (a) not being nationalised and (b) not receiving more than fair treatment with regard to Govern-ment contracts or subsidies. Stephen and Yarrow did not give any definite reply themselves to this invitation. They put the matter to a meeting of the Shipbuilding Conference which recommended that they did not join the Board. Eric Yarrow remained sceptical, explaining that he did not favour "propping up the weak" at the expense of the financially viable companies. He could not bring himself to believe that pledges made by the unions for full co-operation with the management could be relied upon in the long term.

This was the attitude which was making it impossible to achieve complete confidence between unions and management. There was such historically ingrained distrust on both sides, that only a very tough, bristly new broom could sweep it out of the joints and get relations to run smooth.

This is where George Brown played such an invaluable role. Iain Stewart had picked on Oliver Blanford to be his General Manager, but Blanford was employed, under contract, by Jim Stephen. There was just a tentative arrangement for him to be spared to help out. That Hogmanay, Saturday 31 December 1965, when George Brown had interrupted his Scottish holiday to speak to the men at Govan and address the Scottish TUC, Oliver Blanford received a call from Stewart at home, asking him to jump in a car and be round in twenty minutes so that George Brown, who was already late for his STUC conference, could meet him. Blanford whizzed round from Bridge of Weir to Bearsden, breaking records and speed limits.

"Now," said George Brown to those present, including Willie Ross, Secretary of State for Scotland, "how are we going to get Blanford free from Stephen's? I know, invite Jim Stephens round here. I'll talk to him." Another telephone invitation was made. Stephens was on his way. He lived close by.

"I must meet him alone," said Brown, "not in front of you lot." He left the lunch table and hid himself in a room adjoining the entrance hall in Stewart's house. The bell rang, the front door was opened, in walked Stephen and, just by coincidence, out sprang Brown and grabbed him in a friendly bear's embrace.

"This is a matter of national importance," explained Brown, gripping Jim Stephen's shoulders. Stephen agreed to let Blanford go quietly. The shipyard owners had had their first real taste of Government pressure.

Still keen to avoid a complete break with the other yards and with previous yard management, Iain Stewart gave a place on the Board to Jim Lenaghan, who had been Managing Director of Fairfield Shipbuilding and Engineering. This appointment was viewed very badly by the Scottish trade union leaders, who brought it up as the main reason for not wishing to co-operate at a meeting soon after the formation of the new company.

"The lads are still in the hands of the same management," they threw at Stewart as he entered the room. He argued that the key *executive* management was quite new and that the Board, of which Lenaghan, as a skilled Naval Architect, was just one member (not Managing Director and with no executive position), was designed to consider policy from many points of view. The trade union officials accepted this, but Lenaghan had to leave the Board within a few months. Stewart felt that Lenaghan was not able to identify himself effectively with the new project. Lenaghan himself gives two reasons why he left the Fairfields Board about a year earlier than his planned retirement. One was the fact that his presence created a certain awkwardness for the new management, for, as the former Managing Director, he had old members of the staff turning to him when they should have been addressing themselves to the new executives. Secondly, his wife fell seriously ill at that time and did in fact die shortly after he had left the Company to nurse her.

Lenaghan must naturally have resented much of what was said in the new firm, for he had had a strong affection for the old company which he considered had been efficient and unlucky to fall on bad times. It was Lenaghan who had steered Fairfield Shipbuilding and Engineering through the ten-year programme of modernisation which had meant turning the yard upside down, dismantling complete workshops and installing new cranage. He felt he could identify himself with the techniques being introduced as a continuation of the trend he had initiated earlier. The yard had been moving strongly towards better times, he feels, but the Fairfield-Rowan engine works had used up too much of the company's cash reserves. He had met stiff union resistance to new ideas in his era and had been hamstrung by having to keep to the rules made by the Shipbuilding Employers' Federation as a whole.

Lenaghan was the last link with the way things had been run before. Stewart's ship was now definitely steering an uncharted course, and into a storm of opposition from not only the other shipyards but also other industrial leaders, mainly because of the fear of Government intervention, union involvement in management and the prospect of a wages spiral started by higher rates to Fairfield workers.

Under the heading TROJAN HORSE, *British Industry*, the official organ of the Confederation of British Industry, said in its leader:

> If private enterprise believes fervently in private enterprise, as indeed it ought, then it should oppose both Plowden and Fairfield as a matter of principle no matter what the circumstances might be. If it does not, it is indulging in hypocrisy—and dangerous hypocrisy at that.
>
> It is true that in the case of the Fairfield shipyard the issue is blurred by a number of factors— the prospect of modern plant going to waste, men thrown out of work, valuable orders being lost and customers being let down. But surely this is one of the natural hazards of competitive enterprise—the

efficient prevail, the inefficient go to the wall. This, after all, is what building a modern Britain should be all about.

Talk of a brave new world and a grand alliance between Government, private industry and the unions does not alter the fact that a large amount of public money is going to be used to create an artificial situation in which there is a very real danger that the rest of the shipbuilding industry—which has had to put up with and overcome similar problems to those of Fairfield—will have to face subsidised competition and unequal treatment. The industry has professed its anxiety, and with every justification.

The amazing thing about that sort of attitude is that it continued to regard British Shipbuilding as a mighty and proud industry which was facing and *overcoming* problems. In fact the industry was declining so rapidly that it had to be rescued, almost in toto, by Government money in the later Geddes-inspired mergers. British yards were only able to make any worthwhile profits when they were building to Admiralty contracts.

"Put up with and overcome" their problems is a phrase which is seen to be completely empty when applied to the record of British Shipbuilding since the easy immediate post-War days. Between 1957 and 1966 the profit earned on capital employed by shipyards dropped absolutely steadily from 10 per cent to minus 2.6 per cent. The private enterprise shareholders would have been much better off investing their cash in the Post Office Savings Bank.

One of Britain's most famous yards, John Brown's on the Clyde, which built our Queen liners, was making heavy losses year after year, subsidised by the rest of the John Brown engineering group. Many of the shipbuilding companies were not able to stand far enough back to see their

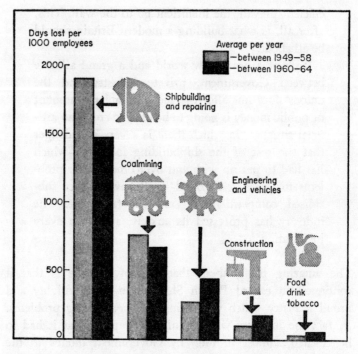

Days lost per 1000 employees

Average per year
—between 1949–58
—between 1960–64

2000

Shipbuilding and repairing

1500

Coalmining

Engineering and vehicles

1000

Construction

500

Food drink tobacco

0

1 SHIPBUILDING CAME TOP OF THE LEAGUE FOR DAYS LOST BECAUSE OF STRIKES

affairs in perspective. When questioned during the preparation of this book, leading figures in shipbuilding still imagined that the loss-making period was merely an unfortunate interval in the proud history of the industry, due mainly to a peculiar world shipping situation and to rising costs at home. The full realisation of the backwardness of construction methods and of management techniques and labour relations in the UK had not struck home. John Rannie, formerly Managing Director of John Brown (Clydebank) Limited, maintains that his yard was a profitable yard, adding only that it was just making losses in the last five years or so. James Lenaghan, previously the Managing Director of Fairfield Shipbuilding, protests that his yard has suffered from the bad publicity after the new Fairfields takeover, but that it was in reality quite efficient. Many Clyde yards insist they were introducing new techniques "gradually." Of these claims, Stewart simply remarks, "Sure, I play golf, so does Arnold Palmer. And he's the professional who knows how to make it pay." Jim Stephen says his yard was experimenting with new methods. He is also proud to point out that the output of UK yards hardly declined at all—in a period when world output rose by several hundred per cent!

Between 1960 and 1964 (according to the Geddes Report) shipbuilding came top of the league for days lost through strikes. It averaged 1500 days a year lost for each 1000 workers, compared with the next highest of about 750 days in coalmining and under 500 in the engineering and vehicle industries. Shipyards had six times more stoppages for each 1000 employees than even the building industry.

From 1954 to 1958, Sweden's shipyards increased output per man from 20.5 tons to 31 tons a year. The performance in British yards actually dropped from 18.8 tons to 18.4 tons per man a year, making us only about half as efficient in the use of labour.

From 1950 to 1960 the output of all world shipbuilders rose from just over three million gross tons to almost twelve million. And Britain's performance? A decrease from $1\frac{1}{2}$ million to $1\frac{1}{4}$ million tons of completed ships. Our share of launched ships in the world hurtled down from almost 50 per cent to around 9 per cent. In 1968 the figures slipped to their lowest ever, with less than a million tons launched, whilst British shipowners actually bought more than two million tons of ships from foreign yards in the same year. In 1968, world output reached a new record level for the third successive year, 16.9 million tons. Britain's share had slipped to as little as 5.3 per cent.

George Brown was not joking when he told Jim Stephen it was a matter of national importance. Someone had to do something.

1950		1955		1960		1965		Estimated 1972–5	
World	British	World	British	World	British	World	British	World	British

2 UK's SHARE OF LAUNCHED SHIPS HURTLED DOWN FROM 50 TO 7 PER CENT

One very unorthodox appointment to the Board of
Fairfields (Glasgow) Limited was Ken Alexander, Professor
of Economics at the University of Strathclyde in Glasgow.
Strange to say, he was not appointed to gain the benefit of
his knowledge of economics, although this came in useful.
Professor Alexander had promised Iain Stewart that if
Stewart were able to found the new company, then he,
Alexander, would undertake to raise finance from the Uni-
versity to sponsor a research project into the effects of the
new management techniques on the shipyard labour.

A researcher, Dr Carson ("Kit") Jenkins, was given the

assignment to record and report on developments inside the yard and he had access to all meetings and every department as he wished. In order to ensure that nothing remained secret from the research project, Stewart gave Alexander a seat on the Board.

Alexander came to be known as the "Universities Director" and he was able to create a link between the shipyard and the academic world, but he was in no way an official representative of the universities. Alexander and Jenkins have together written a book, to be published in the near future, to record for posterity and spread as widely as possible the lessons learnt during the Fairfield Experiment.

Ken Alexander's future works might be even more interesting, because he is serving also as a director of the merger board, Upper Clyde Shipbuilders, and it will be interesting to discover, when the story can be told, how the Fairfields yard and its activities were viewed by people who later came in to weld the five Upper Clyde yards into one big happy family.

Stewart and Professor Alexander came together to discuss industrial relations problems whilst Stewart was President of the Institution of Engineers and Shipbuilders in Scotland. Iain Stewart asked the Professor to give one of the Marlow Lectures which he had inaugurated and Alexander chose as his subject: "Flexibility and Demarcation in Shipbuilding." It was Stewart's involvement with the "Marlow Declaration" which gave rise to the false impression that he was an MRA man or a religious crusader. He is neither. The then MP for Esher, William Robson Brown, had organised a "meeting of minds" (top minds!) at a hotel in Marlow on the Thames to try to discover what was wrong with the British economy. At that concourse were people like the Archbishop of Canterbury, the Archbishop of Westminster, Sir William Carron (now Lord Carron), President of the AEU, Lord Cooper, Lord Collison, Sir Joseph Lockwood, Chairman of EMI, Lord Knollys, Lord Flack, the

Headmaster of Eton and so on. Also invited to attend, as President of the Institution of Engineers and Shipbuilders, was Iain Stewart. The outcome of their deliberations was a statement, or declaration, to the effect that the key to an improved economy was better human relations. One of the Archbishops, (Stewart is not now sure which,) describing the statement to him over cocktails, said, "It is suffering from a certain amount of wind, but I don't want to tamper with it because it will only shift the wind—I am therefore going to sign it."

All these top people gathered together in a London Hotel later to affix their signatures to the Declaration in full view of the Press. Unfortunately, as the arrangements were made by the ecclesiastical press officers, most of the journalists and photographers present were from the church press, with the result that the religious, interdenominational aspect of the whole thing was stressed in all the holy national and parish papers in the realm. Hoping to do something constructive about it all now that he had become a signatory, Stewart founded the series of lectures to enable experts from different walks of life to give their views on human relations in industry. Professor Ken Alexander was one of the lecturers and so later came to find himself really in the thick of the problem.

As half of the share capital of Fairfields was being provided by private investment, it was natural for some private capitalists to join the firm's Board of Directors. Hugh Stenhouse was invited and accepted, throwing his not inconsiderable weight into the job of being a Fairfields Director. He scorned the idea of "representing" any special set of interests, but constantly bore in mind, and bored into everyone else's mind, that the Directors were there to see that what was done was best for Fairfields and not for any particular outside lobby. His theme was that Management, Men and Money all needed each other for industrial success. Although he had invested his Money, he knew a fair amount about the other two items, running his own little empire of insurance and manufacture, and employing 7000 men.

With Stenhouse very much a "lone ranger," someone was still required to represent the interests of Lord Thomson and Sir Isaac Wolfson, who between them had put up a quarter of a million pounds. The man who joined the Board on their behalf was Bill Carron, a signatory to the Marlow Declaration and President of the Amalgamated Engineering Union!

This was an intriguing move by Stewart, for he then had a very qualified spokesman for the engineering unions, able to keep them informed of the value of the Fairfields developments, whilst the official Union Director, Andrew Cunningham, was the Northern District Secretary of the General and Municipal Workers Union. Simultaneously, it has to be borne in mind, Sir William Carron (now Lord Carron) was also a director of the Bank of England, not altogether to be overlooked when so much of the yard's finance had been supplied through the Bank by the Government. Iain Stewart was able to meet all of his requirements without making the Board too cumbersome.

Stenhouse, Carron and Cunningham were only appointed to the Board some months after the launching of the new company. There could be no Union Director until the unions had overcome the difficulties in the way of their investment in a risky financial enterprise. Until the union money was in, as we have seen, the Thomson and Wolfson cash was not unconditionally committed. It was decided to keep private investors away from the Board Room until the unions could be represented.

In the two or three weeks that followed the formation of Fairfields (Glasgow) Limited on 7 January 1965, union after union declared they were not going to participate in the equity. "No boilermakers' cash for Fairfields" announced the headlines, followed later by "Union investment illegal, says ETU." The AEU, the NUGMW and the Draughtsmen and Allied Technicians all withdrew their original promises of cash. The Press and the politicians thought this spelled doom for the yard, knowing that so much of the private investment was dependent upon union participation, but Stewart and George Brown had their little secret document to tide them over whilst Brown got busy on the unions. After multiple secret, semi-secret and public meetings, George Brown found a formula so that Les Cannon of the ETU could state: "The Executive Council of the ETU, having considered in great detail the position of Fairfields, agrees to seek ways and means within the rules of making a financial contribution of up to £50 000 to the finances of this joint venture." The ways and means resulted in a cash loan at 5 per cent interest.

Eventually, five unions had been able to arrange to invest a total of £180 000 by October 1966. The Fairfields shareholding then looked like this:

NUGMW	50 000		
Clerical & Allied Workers	5 000		
Amal Engineering Union	50 000		
Amal Society of Woodworkers	25 000		
	———	130 000 (+ £50 000 loan from	
Stenhouse Investments	50 000	ETU without	
Pennant Finance (Wolfson)	100 000	equity)	
Thomson Scottish	150 000		
H K Salvesen	100 000		
	———	400 000	
		———	530 000
Board of Trade	530 000		530 000
			———
			1 060 000

In addition to this capital (which was mainly used to purchase the assets from the old company's Receiver) the new company was able to call on cash loans from the Board of Trade on standard terms of 7 per cent interest. By November 1966 Fairfields had borrowed an extra £940 000 from that source. During the lobbying of the unions there had been a series of lengthy meetings at the Piccadilly Hotel in London. Discussion had gone on with Jack Cooper, President of the NUGMW (and also another signatory to the Marlow Declaration), Harry Nicholas of the Transport and General Workers Union and leaders from a total of fourteen unions. On one occasion the last man to join the discussions was Dan MacGarvey, President of the Boilermakers. He joined the assembly in a fiery mood and declared, "I'm not signing any statement of intent!" when the purpose of the meeting was outlined to him. The Fairfields people said virtually nothing. Instead the other union executives started in on him and finally a statement of intent to find ways of investing in Fairfields was drafted—by Dan McGarvey. At that stage, far beyond the value of the cash involved was the value of the moral support of the union leaders, publicly and concretely proved by investment. Union co-operation for the new ideas was the vital ingredient for success.

In spite of their reliance upon Government finance, the Fairfield Board refused absolutely to treat the Government as anything more than a shareholder, a shareholder who did not have a majority. On several occasions this point was brought home forcibly to the Government.

The last Director to be appointed to the Fairfields Board was Sir Jack Scamp. As a player of leading parts in the settlement of many industrial disputes, Scamp was regarded by Stewart as a person who could contribute to the two-way communication of ideas on the Board—inwards and out-wards. He wanted Scamp to contribute his experience of industrial relations from other branches of industry and he also wanted Scamp to spread to other industries throughout the country accurate reports of what was being achieved at Fairfields. Stewart had in front of him, constantly, this opportunity of providing a "national proving ground." The stir he was creating on the Clyde had to spread its ripples much further than Govan.

Scamp was appointed to the Board when Wedgwood Benn had taken over the Ministry of Technology, where the Government shares were now lodged. Wedgwood Benn sent a stiff complaint to Stewart via Palmar, the Government Director, demanding to know why he had not been consulted before Scamp's appointment. Stewart, with a very straight bat, sent back the question: "Why?" He made it clear that it was not the custom of a Board to ask its shareholders permission to appoint directors, but merely to inform them after the event. Any shareholder was able to express his views upon a director at the annual general meeting.

A much more striking example of the yard's independence of Government was the refusal to quote for a Government order. The Admiralty wanted to place a T2 type frigate, worth £13.5 million, with Fairfields. The yard said it could be built in sixty months. The Admiralty wanted delivery in fifty-four months. Fairfields maintained this was impossible and Stewart refused to follow the line taken as a matter of course by many other UK yards—make a promise to the Admiralty, get the order and make excuses for late delivery when the time came. This order was placed with another yard and, at the time of going to press with this book, the vessel is already about seven months behind schedule. There seems no possibility of its being delivered even within the "unacceptable" period of sixty months.

The new Board of Fairfields steadfastly refused to accept any possibility of late deliveries. Profitable construction and delivery-to-schedule were the two planks on which the whole company policy rested.

This attitude was demonstrated when Jim Houston the man chosen to take charge of productivity services, was made a member of the full Board. Houston was given tremendous backing by his Board colleagues and, in spite of the tight control of expenditure in order to achieve profitability rapidly, Productivity Services as a department was given the go-ahead for massive investment which probably dwarfs the investment in time and money for these services in any other British company.

It would at first sight appear ridiculous to have literally hundreds of industrial engineers and work study experts dashing around a shipyard employing 3000 men, but the situation was very unusual. The new company could not continue if it did not transform a loss-making activity into a profitable one inside a very short time. The men, the unions and the Government, not to mention the Press and TV, were watching now for results. But productivity bargains, new work systems and controls depend entirely upon accurate information for their success. There was no information available in the yard. Almost every single worker's job had to be timed, the work flow in every department had to be studied and reproduced in diagrammatic form, the system of purchasing had to be overhauled, the timing of supplies, their quantity and their quality had to be checked and fitted into an overall system of operation.

Oliver Blanford and Jim Houston had to introduce techniques of Work Measurement, Quality Control, Value Engineering, Operational Research, Network Analysis, Budgetary Control, Job Evaluation, Investment Appraisal, Management Accounting and Organisation and Methods.

As the Boilermakers' Delegate, Pat Kelly, says: "You name it. Houston brought it."

Jim Houston is fond of relating how the old shipyard system of gathering information was to look at the annual balance sheet produced by the accountants. If it showed a profit, things were OK. If it showed a loss, something was wrong. By then, however, it was impossible to discover exactly what was wrong or how to put it right.

By the time Fairfields had set up its systems, it was possible for the executive management to know at the end of every single week exactly what stage had been reached by every department in the yard; what labour costs were going into the production of any part of a ship and how this compared with budgets; what materials had been received from outside suppliers and how these deliveries compared with the schedules; how much abortive work had been carried out during the week; how much time had been spent on waiting for work; the reasons why a man had had to wait.

Houston insists that the work of a management team can be broken down into two simple categories:

1 Provision of information.
2 Provision of solutions to problems.

Of the two, the provision of information represents seventy-five per cent of management's responsibility. And by this, he means information in two directions:

1 Information for management of the type described above.
2 Information for the workers to assure their co-operation, their intelligent involvement and therefore top efficiency. People, at every level, work best when they know what they are doing and why they are doing it.

Fairfields analysed the whole process of building ships and isolated the major aspects which required the greatest scrutiny. For example, it is commonly stated (especially in defence of the delays to the finishing of the QE2) that sixty per cent of any ship is manufactured outside the shipyard. The engine room compartments, the pumps and auxiliary motors, the electric cables and fittings, the furniture, the sanitary stoneware, the control and electronic apparatus for the bridge, the communications equipment, the dining room, galley, laundry and cargo handling equipment are all bought in by the yard from outside firms. This makes the shipbuilder heavily dependent upon the efficiency of other people.

The yard is also, of course, dependent upon suppliers for the actual construction materials: the steel, the nuts and bolts, the welding electrodes, the sealing materials, the timber and the plastics panels.

Bill Ross was brought in from the printing press manufacturing firm of Goss in Preston to take over the purchasing department of the Fairfields yard. A report of the time describes what was discovered:

> Twenty or thirty people, some of them with very little training or authority, were in effect placing buying orders... It was difficult to get evidence about prices, but we suspected they could be reduced by seven per cent and were even then around fifteen per cent higher than those in the rest of Europe. The buying departments and stores had no records or systems for budgeting, inventory, value analysis, monitoring, progressing or any other form of control. Due to the absence of monitoring and controlling deliveries to meet the existing PERT network programmes, many expensive items of equipment arrived many months ahead of schedule and, conversely, many items failed to arrive in time to meet erection dates.

The new management set up central buying and control systems, to achieve savings of £100 000 in the first year on prices paid compared with those included in the existing tenders. They also appointed two men whose sole job it was to scout round the factories of outside suppliers to ensure that major items were delivered to schedule. They initiated what is called a Cardinal Dates Programme. This sets out very clearly, week by week and month by month, not only what supplies should be received, but what stage the outside manufacturer should have reached in the manufacture of those supplies. This schedule would point out to the Fairfield management the day on which the ships main engines manufacturer should have started machining his cylinders or assembling the engine or should be making the first tests. A letter or telephone call to ask if that stage had been reached on the scheduled day was not considered sufficient. One of the scouts would visit the engine builder and see for himself what progress was being made. Fairfields knew at what point a delay was irretrievable. They had to make sure that urgent action was taken in advance of any such "disaster dates" in order to get the component back into place on the Cardinal Date Programme. Fairfields, when they took an order and guaranteed a delivery date for a ship, accepted complete responsibility for it, with no mental reservations about possible delay due to late arrival of supplies or strikes in their own yard. They considered that any shipowner placing an order should be able to rely on the shipyard management to control its own labour force and its own subcontractors.

At the same time, Fairfields also defined the responsibilities of the shipowner. There was to be no vague "to owner's satisfaction" wording of the contract. There was to be no changing of minds about design or layout of the ship after the steel had been ordered and the construction begun, unless the owner was prepared to negotiate a new price to cover the extra costs and a new delivery date to take account of the change in schedules.

For example, there is a great deal of controversy over the delay to the container ship which the Fairfields yard took on for Overseas Containers Limited, OCL. This was one of six similar ships, with the other five being built by West German yards. The Fairfields schedule could not get started because the drawings for the design were not forwarded to them by the German yard. Without drawings a shipbuilder cannot order steel, cannot prepare any detailed work schedule.

The drawings should have been received in September 1967, but nothing had arrived by early March 1968. By that time, Oliver Blanford was able to prepare a fully documented report for his Board, (which was also presented to the merged UCS Board,) explaining how the delay had eliminated all the contingency time built into the original schedule, how it would affect the plans for the future and what action would be needed to put things right. The remedies included: Revision of the drawing office programme, allocation of nine additional draughtsmen to the office, six additional loftsmen (for preparation of the templates for the steel plate cutting), subcontracting of 2300 tons of steel to the neighbouring Linthouse yard (formerly Stephen's) and introduction of a double-shift period of construction between May and October 1968.

In addition, a Fairfield draughtsman was actually sent off to Germany to sit in the German drawing office to grab the urgently required drawings and clarify any obscure aspects of the designs and notations.

In the previous January a *force majeure* letter had already been despatched giving extremely early notice of the delay which would be inevitable if the German drawings were not expedited.

The Fairfields Board approved all these actions, including a second *force majeure* letter before handing over the yard to the newly formed Upper Clyde consortium. That action was taken more than twelve months before the ship in question was due to be launched.

During the two years that Fairfields (Glasgow) Limited was in operation, the yard built six ships. Three of these were ships already under construction when the old firm had gone bankrupt. The other three, whose construction had begun under Stewart's regime and had been seen right through by the new team, were delivered as follows: the first was exactly on time to the very day; the second was delivered one day early; the third was delivered one week early. This was badly needed by the owners, Reardon Smith of Cardiff, because of the closure of the Suez Canal which upped freight rates so profitably for shipowners. Reardon Smith, therefore, subsequently placed orders for two further ships with Fairfields. This is the highest accolade of recommendation for a yard, especially when Fairfields had made a profit on the first orders and were quoting for a good profit on the new ones.

To readers associated with other industries, this emphasis on quoting for orders at a profit may sound curious, for what could be more natural in business than quoting for a job in order to make a profit on doing the job! But this was not the routine practice in Britain's shipyards. A large number of orders for ships were taken on at a loss-making price solely to keep the yards alive until something better turned up. As nothing better turned up for such a lengthy period and the banks refused to go on financing losses, many yards could not live off fat or parent company subsidies any longer and had to close their doors.

The Fairfield venture aimed to prove that budgeting to make a loss was not necessary if radical changes were made to methods of work, internal relations and leadership in the industry. Most of the ideas brought in by the new team were "old hat" to sophisticated industries. This would be confirmed by executives such as Reg Ingram who was Comptroller or Company Secretary, brought in from Penguin Books. The innovation which caused such a stir was the introduction of all these management techniques en masse into the shipbuilding industry, where aspects of productivity methods had only been trickling through, and generally meeting fierce resistance from unions and managers.

Fairfield Shipbuilding and Engineering Company Limited, the old firm, had introduced the sophisticated PERT system of production and supplies control, but it is a system which can only be effective if fed constantly with up-to-the-minute accurate information on progress and there were no auxiliary systems operating to collect this information.

Stewart made a clean sweep of the Fairfields table. His team then systematically examined each part of the process of running a shipyard and built a totally new structure of management, communications, pay, construction techniques, training, purchasing and discipline. No one was allowed to hark back to the old system for justification of anything. Everything had to be justified on its contribution to the new, profit-making Fairfields.

One of the main stanchions of this new edifice was Discipline. "The men were over a barrel," Stewart is not afraid to confess, "and I intended to keep them there until they understood our new techniques and trusted them and until the yard was running as I wanted it to run. It was a case of 'Follow me, be prepared to listen and learn and share in the profitable future, or go and work somewhere else.' That is how I put it to them, in my speeches at the Lyceum Cinema."

In order to maintain this pressure of discipline, Stewart omitted one thing which all sophisticated industries would consider the main essential. He had no marketing or sales organisation in the whole new company. He expressly made no attempt to obtain orders until the yard had been totally and tightly reorganised, for he wanted to use the precipice of unemployment to keep the men on the narrow path he needed them to follow.

Besides, he could not possibly promise any firm delivery dates or quote any reliable prices until the new agreements on productivity and interchangeability had been completely settled, until the threat of strikes had been eliminated and the efficiency of ship construction improved.

In the two years of their operation, no sales team or department was required, for exactly at the right moments opportunities for orders cropped up, just sufficiently to keep the yard balanced on its chosen tightrope walk. Stewart was confident that once the world saw what Fairfields was able to offer under guarantee, then sales would be no problem. Through the Press and TV the world kept itself very fully informed of what went on in the yard, representing the greatest ever publicity campaign mounted by a shipyard, any- where in the world, and completely free of charge!

Without being solicited, enquiries came in from owners, asking if Fairfields could quote them for ships. The yard was able to pick and choose, fitting orders in to exactly the slots prepared for them by the new team.

Systematically the labour force was cut down in the first six months by about 750 men, the remainder were retrained and then loaded up to the brim with work and confidence. In the end, they got to like being "over a barrel," like an athlete who appreciates the punishment he suffers in training to keep on top.

Even the mixed bag of personalities on the Board had to be controlled and welded into a team to make the most of their different strengths and experiences. Stewart always in- vited them all to dinner the night before each Board Meet- ing. Over dinner and afterwards the Directors could let fly at each other with invectives, table thumping, sarcasm or plain bloody-mindedness. By the next morning, all excess heat had been generated, a concensus of feelings and thoughts had been gathered during exchanges which had caused no lasting harm, and decisions could be reached speedily and unanimously. In its two years existence, the Board never had to come to a vote to make a decision. Each member had learnt the night before the extent to which he was pushing a minority opinion. Each had had a chance to mould his own ideas under the pressure of ideas from the others. The dinners were another good investment.

Chapter six

Goodbye to the Grapevine

When 1000 employees of the Blyth Dry Docks and Ship-building Company Limited, of Blyth, on the north-east coast of England, were on their second week's holiday in August 1966, they each received a letter telling them not to report back to work but to go instead to the local employment exchange. They had lost their jobs. The yard was bankrupt.

It was what one might call an example of poor communications within a company. It is the kind of thing which can lead towards poor industrial relations.

"Do a Fairfields for us!" cried the Blyth shop stewards.

Fairfields had already become a symbol of a new deal in less than eight months. At the time the Blyth men were receiving their summer holiday surprise, the Fairfields shop stewards were sitting as guests at the launching of *British Commodore*, as fully informed of the state of the yard as any of the directors present. In fact, some Fairfields shop stewards knew more about Fairfields than the Blyth directors knew about Blyth. The information-gathering systems and the information-giving systems had been implemented. It was these which made the yard swing along in unison. No one, from the office girls and apprentices to the foremen, shop stewards and Executive Directors, was left to grope along in the dark.

The main Board made policy decisions, but the yard itself was run by an Executive Management Committee headed by the General Manager, Oliver Blanford. On this Committee were Jim Houston, Director of Productivity Services, and the heads of each main department, Buying, Accounts, Design, Joinery, Outfitting (fitting out the ships after the launch), Machinery, Pipework, Plant, Steelwork, Public Relations and Contracts (each ship under construction had a Ship Contracts Manager to oversee it). Iain Stewart kept well away from the daily running of the yard and never ever went on board any of the ships being built. He made it clear to the men that Oliver Blanford was in command.

When the Executive Management Committee met, there were also three extra people present. These were the Yard Convener of Shop Stewards, Alex McGuinness, and two other stewards, the Boilermakers' Convener, George Gray, and the AEU Convener, John Airlie. They were observers, able to participate in the discussions but without any vote on resolutions. Their lack of voting powers was an arrangement which was put forward by the unions themselves in order to maintain a distinction between management and union responsibilities. It was considered dangerous to blur the differences between two separate sets of duties.

The three shop stewards were issued with all the same material, the facts and the figures, which were made available to the full members of the committee. Decisions were made and then, when the meeting was terminated, each department head went back to report immediately to his junior managers. Simultaneously throughout the yard, all the work study, recruitment, wages, design and other managers and foremen were put in the picture about new developments, failings, successes, administrative changes or other announcements.

These middle managers then, in their turn, passed on the

information in meetings to their working staffs, to the draughtsmen, to the industrial engineers, to the steelworkers, the crane drivers, the welders and the joiners. It was an essential part of the system that everyone had to be informed of what was going on by his immediate superior, so that the proper chain of command was preserved and the proper respect created for the junior managers and foremen.

Meanwhile, the three shop stewards were able to put the other stewards in the picture so that if the men were at all unclear or disgruntled at any decisions reported down to them, there was someone in their union to whom they could turn and who was so completely aware of the reasoning behind the decisions that misunderstandings could be avoided.

The system sounds laborious, but in fact the time taken between the taking of executive management decisions and the information being given personally and in detail to the tea girls and apprentices and gatemen was one hour. In that time all 3500 employees in the yard were fully briefed on the latest, official news. No unofficial grapevine ever worked more quickly.

As a result, it was the men who were able themselves to give the news of orders or Board appointments to their wives and families. They no longer had to rely upon the local fishmonger to keep them in the picture.

All Press Releases and other public announcements were first checked with the shop stewards Convener before going out, not only to inform him but to check the union reaction to any statement to be made public. Furthermore, there was the vital channel of communication, *Fairfield News*. This was edited by Bill Hawkins. The first issue of *Fairfield News* appeared the moment the yard was taken over by the new management and it appeared regularly each month for the whole operating life of Fairfields (Glasgow) Limited. It introduced itself with the inevitable house journal fanfare:

THE VOICE OF FAIRFIELDS

The reason for the birth of *Fairfield News* is simple. Its primary function will be one of communication. We also hope that it will encourage a community feeling among Fairfield people and will contribute to understanding and goodwill in the yard itself. If this spreads outside the yard then so much the better.

We intend that *Fairfield News* will become the voice of Fairfields (Glasgow) Limited. Not the voice of management. Not the voice of men. But the voice of a company where its people are dovetailed into a single unit striving for better working conditions, better pay, more mutual respect, and the satisfaction which comes from a job well done.

The Fairfield experiment is already famous for producing such a splendid and mixed variety of critics and cynics. We are not really concerned about these people.

We are concerned with building ships. Building good ships. Building them on time. Building them at the right price.

Fairfield craftsmen and works people do not need instructions from Japan or Sweden on the fundamentals of shipbuilding.

But most of all management must play its part. The company is recruiting the new skills required to supplement those which we already have.

All we have to do is work together.

We intend to do just that.

Fairfield News lived up to its claims. As one Boilermaker member put it: "Everything that happened, Bill had it in that paper. Of course, Stephen's Yard had *Linthouse News,* but that paper was too full of the Stephens."

Fairfield News was the mouthpiece of anyone in the company who wished to communicate something to all the others in the company. Shop stewards, union delegates or work study specialists, all had their articles published, alongside reports on progress from the Chairman or the Managing Director. The yard was kept aware of its role as "national proving ground" with continuous reprints in *Fairfield News* of complete articles from papers such as the *Daily Mirror*, *The Times* and from the shipping journals.

The paper served, too, as a source of reference material, for the Chairman's policy speeches and promises, diagrams of Management structure, the exact terms of Union-Management Agreements were all reproduced, to be kept as a permanent record by the employees. When Kit Jenkins joined the yard to carry out the research project, a question-and-answer interview with Professor Alexander explained to everyone exactly what the research project was all about and included a photograph of Jenkins plus his yard office number so that he was available to receive information from any-one. To underline the principle of free and unprejudiced communication, the second issue of *Fairfield News*, in March 1966, carried statements specially contributed by local parliamentary candidates from Govan and Craigton, giving their views on the Fairfield proving ground. There were two Conservative candidates, two Labour, one Communist and one Scottish National. This was a different world from the one in which local socialist MPs were not allowed access to meet the men.

Again to avoid the flavour of a "management propaganda sheet," a price of 3d was put on the *Fairfield News*. It was not handed out free. Over 70 per cent of the yard employees subscribed.

Communications are vital in battles, and the Fairfield management team had to treat their task almost as a military exercise. Although there were cynics, scoffers and attackers hostile to the experiment in the business, political and in-dustrial world, the main enemy was time. It was evident

101

that Fairfields (Glasgow) Limited had to show profitable results very rapidly, for patience, and with it cash, would soon run out if there was nothing concrete to show the workers, the unions, the private investors and the changing Government Ministers.

There was, therefore, no question of gradual education of the workers into new methods. Co-operation was essential right from the start. Co-operation depended upon everyone knowing what was expected of him and what he was going to get out of it as a reward. Jim Houston once decided to explain what Measured Daywork meant to every person in the company. During four days and nights, he met every shift in every department. He talked with sixteen groups, each of about 200 to 250 men, for one and a half to two hours each time. He described what they had to achieve, told them how their section fitted into the whole picture and then answered questions. In his turn, he learned about their working conditions, their fears and their hopes.

One day, Hugh Stenhouse, soon after becoming a member of the Board, rang Oliver Blanford and asked if it would be possible to be shown round the yard. "Certainly," replied Blanford, "shall we meet tomorrow morning at seven-forty?"

"Why," queried Stenhouse, "what's happening?"

Nothing special was happening. It was just that the Managing Director and every member of the Executive Management Committee made a point of arriving at the yard before the men. Blanford visited a different section each morning and was there to greet the workers as they came in.

Although Stewart left the running of the yard to his executives, he did make sure that the men all knew what he personally expected of them and what the aim of the company was. He kept up the enthusiasm and the sense of personal involvement with regular mass meetings at the Lyceum Cinema. Located just along the road from the yard, it dated from the grand era of plush cinemas and could hold several thousand people at a time. A cinema meeting (there were five in the two years) was regarded as an integral part of the working day. The men were paid for attending and so were checked in by tellers at the main entrance. The Chairman of the company, Iain Stewart, did not chair the meeting. He was simply the main speaker. He himself pointed out on one occasion: "You will note that Mr Blanford is in the chair—this is right and proper because he is the Chairman of the Management Committee, and is therefore the real boss in Fairfields Shipyard."

In his speeches, Stewart reviewed the progress made, detailed aspects which needed improvement and described the plans for the next stage of the experiment. He used the occasions to make the workers realise they were playing an important part in a very significant venture.

> Like it or not [he said], we are living in a gold-fish bowl and I don't suppose that any company in Britain is subjected to so much public scrutiny and this makes our job that much more difficult. We cannot afford to make the same mistakes twice and everything we do must be seen to be done well and to be successful. So also must our attitudes in every sector of the organisation be seen to be in line with the pledges which were given in December.

To stave off feelings of impatience and to gain further co-operation, he gave the background to the negotiations on new productivity agreements:

> With the boilermakers we have negotiated the abolition of PBR (payment by results), the con-solidation of earnings, the acceptance of method study, plus flexibility between shipwrights and riggers. With the mechanics we are discussing

the very progressive agreement about flexibility and talks are going ahead on similar lines with the blacksmiths, the ETU and so on. So far as the wage structure is concerned we knew it was bad when we started, but one could not have imagined that we would have inherited such a dog's dinner—in the sheet iron shop, for instance, we have a dozen or more different rates applying, and can you imagine a better breeding ground for discontent and differentials!

I also therefore call for a firm and unshaken belief that at the end of our proving period we will not only have come to terms with these innumerable anomalies, but will be operating the most efficient shipyard in Britain.

In that event we will also have set new standards in co-operation, in productivity and modern methods which will act as a model for many other industries.

You can in fact make an immediate contribution to this philosophy by cutting absenteeism and lateness down to a level which could be the envy of every shipyard in the country. Some sections I am glad to say have already done so. Let us hope that next time we review our progress this inexcusable shortcoming will not be in evidence.

Far from being demagogic tub-thumping, as some critics have claimed, the tone of Stewart's delivery was more like that of a Headmaster at Speech Day, recording successes, creating the team spirit and admonishing backsliding. With spectacles half-way down his nose so he could look down at his speech through them and out at the massed audience above them, Stewart read his words carefully into the standing microphone on the Lyceum's stage, before the heavy drops of the cinema curtain.

His first speech was the one given on 27 December 1965, after that last-minute Christmas rescue. By the time of his second cinema appearance, 27 April 1966, Stewart had many proofs that his idealist philosophy could be applied in practice. He was already able to say that the five-year proving period might be shortened because of the rapid progress made. But he ended with a reminder that there was much to be done and only the "believers" could be tolerated.

> I would like to say one brief word to anyone who may be here this morning who does not believe in what we are trying to do or does not wish to be associated with it. There is no reason at all why you should feel obliged to stay and we will help you to find alternative employment. But let the rest of us continue the good work of progress, let us weld this organisation into one which has real unity of purpose and let us continue to convert our critics, in addition to confounding those who do not wish us well.

At the end of his speeches, hand microphones were passed around the auditorium, enabling anyone to ask a question. One questioner asked when the workers would be allowed to buy shares! No one could complain at Fairfields that there was insufficient communication between men and management.

The basic problem which had faced Stewart was one which impeded the progress of almost every industry in Britain. This was the lack of freedom for management to manage without the threat of strikes against changes. The communications systems, the discipline of publicity and the precipice of unemployment, the leadership and the dynamism all had to create the situation in which real and reliable agreements could be signed with the unions, accepted at every level—on the shop floor, in the Shop Stewards Committee, at the Scottish TUC and by the leaders of the Confederation of Shipbuilding and Engineering Unions at York.

As Ford Motor Company has found out recently, agreements are not agreements unless the signatures to them really do have the backing of everyone who will be affected by them. Stewart did not want mere pieces of paper. He wanted documents which summarised, without possibility of misinterpretation, all the procedures which the men and the unions had accepted and pledged themselves to recognise. Individual agreements were negotiated with separate unions in the yard to cover special needs. In each case these were vetted by shop stewards, local delegates and any other interested parties. A "revolutionary" agreement was signed by the national leaders of thirteen unions in the Fairfields Boardroom on 2 June 1966. It was published *in toto*, in advance of the signing, in *Fairfield News* in May. There was no possibility of anyone in the yard, at any level, complaining after the event that they were ignorant of the contents. Everyone had a chance to study the details and make approaches to union or management long beforehand.

Signatories to this agreement were the AEU, the Boilermakers, the Woodworkers, the ETU, the General and Municipal Workers, the Sheet Metal Workers and Coppersmiths, the Plumbing Trades Union, the Amalgamated Society of Painters and Decorators, the Transport and General Workers, the United Patternmakers, the Draughtsmen's and Allied Technicians' Association, the Association of Supervisory Staffs, Executives and Technicians, the Clerical and Administrative Workers and, of course, Fairfields (Glasgow) Limited. (In the same issue of *Fairfields News* was a photograph of Pat Kelly of the Boilermakers and Jim Houston of Fairfields signing an interchangeability agreement, permitting redundant sheet iron workers to be absorbed within the platers department. Kelly is quoted as saying: "The negotiations have been going on since early March and the agreement means that Fairfields

are leading the field on Clydeside." Fairfields had obviously
been busy!)

The Procedure Agreement signed by the thirteen union
leaders was described as "historic" and "revolutionary."
Although parts of it had been accomplished in other industries, the agreement was indeed unique and a breakthrough seen in the context of labour relations in British
shipbuilding. There were two important innovations. One
was the Central Joint Council which was to serve as a union-
management forum to settle problems jointly. The other was
a detailed Procedure for the negotiation of pay and
grievances.

The Central Joint Council consisted of three executives
from the biggest union in the yard, the Boilermakers
Society, and one executive from each of the other twelve
unions; and three executives from Fairfields management.
The Company had the right to appoint the Chairman of the
Council. Meetings could be called by either side with two
weeks notice, but it was statutory for the CJC to meet at
least once every three months. It could be called to discuss
any matter affecting employees of the Company or affecting
the employers' interest. It was the responsibility of the CJC
to negotiate all agreements in connection with basic wage
applications and common conditions of employment.

This meant that there was an inner "parliament" where
unions and management could thrash out difficulties
regularly, avoiding the "festering" condition of problems
which gives rise to deep resentment in industry. Shop
stewards were being recognised by the Company as responsible individuals with the right to make a case for their men
in the best possible conditions for a fair hearing.

Parallel with the Central Joint Council, the agreement
laid down a clear, exclusive Procedure to settle disputes. If
the CJC was the "parliament," the Procedure might be regarded as setting up the "Courts of Justice," with series of
steps taking any dispute to higher and higher authority, each

107

capable of arranging a settlement without the need for strike weapons to be used. The procedure was as follows:

1   Meeting between the individual with a grievance and his foreman or departmental head, the man's shop steward being present if desired by the employee. If the grievance concerns more than one man, then the shop steward represents them. If the grievance concerns more than one union, then the Convener represents them and negotiates with the Personnel Manager.

2   If the first-stage meeting fails to produce a solution satisfactory to both sides, then a *Local Official Conference* is called, to be convened as quickly as possible and normally not longer than ten days after requested. The District official of the union concerned here meets with one or more senior managers of the Company to try to solve the problem which has arisen.

3   Should agreement still not be reached, then either side (the Company or the Executive Committee of the Union or Unions) can refer the matter a stage further to a *Scottish Conference*, where two or more officials of the unions, nominated by the Central Joint Council, and two senior managers of the Company, will come to the table. Their decision will be final and binding upon all concerned.

4   However, if there is still a measure of discontent over this decision, union members are permitted to go even further if they regard the matter as "of grave importance." They can ask their unions to call an emergency conference to be attended by the firm's Managing Director and other senior managers, Trade Union Officials and also members of the Conciliation Branch of the Ministry of Labour (as it was then). "No stoppage, overtime

ban, or other limitation on production of work shall take place until this point has been reached, and the procedure exhausted." (See Appendix 2.)

Now there had been, of course, some simpler forms of procedure in earlier days, but the tendency had been for management to drag its feet. The Fairfield Convener, Alex McGuinness, remembered one instance when it took two years seven months to receive an answer to a query in the old Fairfields, where he had also been Convener of Shop Stewards. "Failure to agree," say the unions, "was the management formula for delaying wage increases."

The new Procedure meant that at the outside it would only take three months from the first sign of a grievance to the "grave matter" Conference, with every possible chance of agreement at each stage of negotiation. Furthermore, to prove that neither side had anything to gain by introducing delaying tactics, the following formula was incorporated in the Procedure Agreement: "The settlement arrived at during such negotiations shall be back-dated to take effect for the first complete pay week after the date of the meeting [with the Personnel Services Manager]."

It was part of the agreement that there would be no stoppages to act as threats during negotiations, so management would be able to look upon strikes as cancelling the previous period of negotiation when the back-dating period was totted up.

On the same day as the signing of this agreement, 2 June, the Boilermaker's Society signed another agreement with Fairfields, abolishing demarcation between the different trades within the union. John Chalmers, General Secretary of the Boilermakers Society, said: "It goes far beyond anything which has taken place in any other British yard. It marks the end of demarcation. It is a far-reaching agreement, representing the complete relaxation of the present working practices within the steel trades in this yard."

The following day the newspapers had one of those nicely juxtaposed situations to make a story. The *Daily Telegraph* commented, "Clydeside's shipbuilding industry provided two strange contrasts yesterday. On the south side of the river agreements were signed which hailed ending strikes and demarcation disputes. On the north side, workers rejected pleas by their union officials that they should allow seventy-eight men whose work had run out to be taken on temporarily in other jobs at John Brown's yard."

The Fairfields Agreement acknowledged the Unions and Shop Stewards as working partners in the yard. One clause even offered to collect union dues by deducting them straight from the wages and handing them over, in a lump sum, to the union official. (It would save a considerable amount of working time every Friday in the yard.) This was not taken up, however, because the shop stewards felt that it would tend to break their own personal contact with the individual members of the union. (The stewards also received a commission on the dues they collected.) Fairfields agreed that "the Company requires and will encourage its employees to be members of the appropriate trade union. The company will not recruit an employee who is not a member of his appropriate trade union and will refer the new employee to the appropriate shop steward/trade union representative."

The article in *Fairfield News* by Pat Kelly, the local District Delegate, pointed out that:

> Worker and Management relations have certainly improved over the past few months. In the new conference room you can sit down, relax and have good discussion, whereas in the past you were never sure of not being arrested outside the gate, as sometimes when the police saw a Delegate paying out money to Stewards they were not sure whether he was a union man, a moneylender or a

bookie! We can sigh with relief that this embarrassment has been removed.

Kelly also stated in print, in the company's own paper, that "it is important we keep this yard healthy. Certainly, once we get new orders we will make claims for wages and better conditions to the new Management." Everyone definitely knew where their interests lay! The unions had not opted out of their main role. Nor had management handed over any of its own rights and duties (as some critics maintained at the time). The Procedure Agreement also contained a clause to the effect that "the Trade Unions recognise the right and duty of the Company to select, appoint and promote employees, Foremen/Departmental Heads and Managers at the Company's discretion and make the decisions required to run the business as a commercially viable unit."

The unions now had such a weight of official responsibility in the yard and there were so many revolutionary projects to negotiate, that the Convener of the Shop Stewards Committee only occasionally had time to drive his crane. He was spending over five hours a day on union business. The Fairfields management made another revolutionary gesture by inviting the unions to appoint a man to be a full-time Convener, paid the full rate by the company to handle union business. This was the first time such an appointment was ever made in a British shipyard. Alec McGuinness of the General and Municipal Workers, a crane driver, was voted into the post. He was provided with his own office in the yard and telephone. For the first time union delegates and executives from outside could make immediate contact with the yard Convener. It was not many years earlier that McGuinness had found it difficult to get a job in the yard, for, as an active shop steward, he believed himself to be on a blacklist and was refused employment when he applied. It had taken union pressure to force the Company to reconsider his case.

111

As shop stewards explain, "we were always thought of as dangerous agitators with black cloaks and bombs. Now, we had respect and so we could negotiate on behalf of the men like reasonable people with reasonable people."

The union point of view was, by August 1966, represented on the Board, at Executive Management Committee meetings and officially at shop steward level. There was a logical procedure for the settlement of disputes and an agreed ban on strikes and go-slows. There was already a wide measure of agreement on the abolition of demarcation in return for an advance of "royalties" on productivity increases. The men were able to communicate without hindrance with their foremen, departmental heads, shop stewards and even the yard Chairman. Everyone was fully informed on Company news and plans and performance. Facilities were available for union conferences on the premises and communication was possible between yard stewards and local officials.

That is why the atmosphere amongst the workers was so noticeably enthused with a spirit of hope for the future when the new Fairfields launched its first ship, *British Commodore*, that August. When the ship actually floated on the Clyde, even the Directors and Managers were able to share that same spirit of optimism. Iain Stewart could confidently tear to little pieces the stand-by speech he had prepared to apologise in the event of failure.

Chapter seven

The Shipyard "University"

'When we weren't working, we were teaching," Jim Houston says of Fairfields (Glasgow) Limited. In their two short years they retrained more men at Fairfields than the whole of the Government retraining centres in Scotland.

Professor Alexander's full-time yard researcher, Kit Jenkins, said in his report at the end of ten months operations:

> The Productivity Services Department is probably unique in British shipyards; the composition of its staff is also unusual. The senior positions are held by men recruited from outside the company, but the junior positions of the Work Study Section were filled by people recruited from the existing work force in the yard.
>
> When the company decided to recruit Industrial Engineers and Analytical Estimators the positions were advertised in the yard. There was a very good response to the advertisement and all applicants were given intelligence and aptitude tests to determine their fitness for training. Those men who were selected as potential Industrial Engineers were put on a ten weeks training course and the Analytical Estimators on a four weeks course. In-

113

struction was given mainly by the Industrial Engineering senior staff with the assistance of a few guest lecturers.

The cost of training was a minimum of £230 for each Industrial Engineer and £104 for Analytical Estimators. In all, it is estimated that a minimum of £12 000 has been spent on training and developing talented people within the yard up to 1 December 1966. One of the most interesting aspects of this scheme is the opportunity it gives to the tradesman and unskilled worker to branch out into new industrial fields.

None of the trainees failed to complete the courses and none have failed to meet the "on the job" training requirements. This investment in men for management is necessary for the future. In addition to the time and money spent on training new talent, top management has not been slow to recognise the abilities of many of the older clerical, administrative and shipyard staff.

Jenkins then made a comment which hints, in a sentence, at a great tragedy of wasted ability.

For too long much of this talent had been neglected and many new appointments have given new enthusiasm to people who were becoming the victims of neglect and apathy.

How many men had in past years grown up in the yards and found inadequate outlet for their talents which would have engendered bitterness and resentment? Just as management throws up its hands in horror at "suicidal" moves made by unions or wildcat strikes which will jeopardise the future of a yard's jobs, so do the men suffer deeply when they see the disastrous results of uninspired or backward management. On the Clyde there are now many men in responsible management positions who found the way from the shopfloor suddenly lighted by the new opportunities offered by a new management. This was not the generation-long hard slog which produced some managers who kept to the old methods they had always practised. It was a rapid transition from manual labour to planning and supervision responsibilities accomplished by instruction in the most up-to-date techniques. The almost automatic resistance to out-siders carrying stopwatches, which causes so much labour trouble in many industries, was avoided because the majority of the men carrying stopwatches at Fairfields were men who themselves two or three months before had been doing the work they were measuring. They were trusted and accepted by their mates in the yard and they themselves were endowed with a conscientiousness that only a new chance in life can inspire.

Lord Carron (formerly Sir William Carron, President of the Amalgamated Engineering Union) says he was greatly impressed as he watched these developments from his posi-tion on the Fairfields Board. He saw a magnificent combina-tion of the old engineering skills with new working tech-niques. The old skills were preserved whilst the old fears were eliminated.

Planeloads of Fairfields men were flown down to London Airport, driven into the Surrey countryside and, in the set-ting of one of Britain's most glorious stately homes, Esher Place, they studied new productivity techniques at residential courses. Esher Place is the ETU Training College run by Jock Haston, the Union's Education Officer. He was asked if he would allow Fairfields to use the magnificent facilities there to train shop stewards and deputies, because Jim Houston wanted the men to feel they were still "on union territory." There was a danger that the stewards might resist "brainwashing by management," as some of the unions from other yards liked to call the retraining.

Fairfields was the first outside organisation to use the ETU centre for its own courses. The scheme was launched on 2 May 1966, in the company's very early days. It was not a cheap exercise, but it was another pioneering investment with a keen eye on early returns.

The scheme caused a national stir. "Shop stewards fly in for millionaire course," shouted the *Sun*; "Fairfield men go to school." "*WELL DONE IAIN*," announced the *Daily Record*. "Shop stewards are going back to school to try to get their firm out of the mire," explained the *Daily Mirror*, whilst the *Financial Times* went so far as to say:

> At the Electrical Trades Union Staff College, Esher (Surrey), this week, history is being made in union integration. Twenty-six shop stewards and deputies from shipbuilders Fairfields (Glasgow) are attending the first of three courses in work study appreciation. What is unique is that a shipbuilding company is doing this (at a cost of £6000) and the ten craft unions represented at the yard are all participating. Mr J. D. Houston, a Director of Fairfields, told the *Financial Times* last night that it was important to remove any fear the men might have about the modern techniques the new top management proposes to introduce. The aim is to train one in twenty of the 3000 people (including forty-nine shop stewards) involved in work study and ancillary subjects. Much of this is being done at Esher, to avoid any possible stigma of brain-washing. Mr Houston said it took only three minutes to get unanimous approval from all the unions for this venture.

Every precaution was taken to proclaim the honest intentions of the project, for there was such historic suspicion on the Clyde of any moves towards union-management integration.

116

Houston invited the local delegates of trades unions to join the Esher courses as observers and the invitation was accepted. For example, on the third course, held from 27 June to 1 July 1966, there were three full time delegates in attendance, James Anderson, the District Organiser of the Amalgamated Society of Woodworkers, A R Peacock, Shipbuilding Officer of the General and Municipal Workers Union and J Black of the Electrical Trades Union.

The men on the course were worked extremely hard, with sixty hours of study and lecture and discussion sessions. They were paid a full week's pay in advance of the trip, with two nights and a Sunday overtime pay included and £3 out-of-pocket expenses. Their sessions included the objectives of Productivity Services, explanations of the purposes and methods of Work Study, the intricacies of Measured Day-work systems, the applications and operation of Network Analysis and the means of negotiating Work Study and Productivity agreements. Talks were given by members of the Fairfields management, executives from PA Management Consultants and executives of the ETU College. The Fairfields speakers included Jim Houston and Professor Alexander. Houston was spending a hectic day at the yard in Glasgow, flying down late afternoon to London so that he could participate in the evening discussion groups, and then flying back in the early hours of the morning to start another day at the yard, almost every day of each of the courses.

The courses were called "Work Study Appreciation Courses." They did not attempt to train the shop stewards in work study, but merely explained the terminology and the objectives and the potential benefits so that the union representatives could understand the significance of what the Industrial Engineers and Work Study specialists would be doing in the yard in the coming months. The time and money invested at Esher by Fairfields was simply an exercise to avoid misunderstanding and to gain union co-operation.

117

The two hundred or so Industrial Engineers who actually did the new work were recruited through advertisements in *Fairfield News* and on the yard notice boards. They went through intensive one month and three-month training courses in Scotland to equip them for their new jobs. At the same time, Fairfields took another step to avoid possible wrangles and labour troubles. They included in the intensive training courses a number of workers who would not actually be employed as Industrial Engineers. These people were nominated by the yard workers, two from each main department, to act as Workers Representatives. In any dispute between a worker and the Industrial Engineer measuring and studying his methods of work, the worker could always turn to one of these Representatives for an explanation of what was going on. The Workers Representative was as fully trained as the Industrial Engineer himself, so that he could advise, with authority, on whether or not the worker's complaint was justified.

This scrupulous preparation of the ground meant that the massive new team of experts could set to work on their gigantic task of measuring and timing every aspect of the shipbuilding operation without any hostile confrontation with the workforce. The investment in time and money and manpower for these productivity preparations was enormous, proportionately the biggest investment of its kind in British industrial history. Fairfields probably paid more than a quarter of a million pounds in wages alone in twelve months for the productivity staff. But it was an invisible asset which was geared to pay for itself in the production of ships more quickly with less manpower, at a greatly reduced cost. These were t he only results which could save not only Fairfields, but British Shipbuilding, and Iain Stewart and his Board saw this kind of investment as the only way to realise these results inside an acceptable period of time.

Productivity Services can be as vague or as specific as the

people behind it. Fairfields were very specific and planned and trained to achieve the following results.

Programme control was introduced in order to ensure that all aspects of production were planned and supervised to produce ships on time without waste of labour or materials.

Industrial engineering was the tool or technique employed to examine actual methods of work and the equipment involved so that management could know exactly what standard of performance was to be expected. Costings and work estimates could be accurate when quoting for ships and when planning future work loading for the yard as a whole.

Organisation and methods was a section of Houston's outfit intended to improve administrative and office procedures and simplify the paper work. (Productivity Services can drown itself in paper work if not controlled and there is a distinct danger, also, that the new systems will go completely astray if the individuals from the shop floor up to the senior management are baffled by the documents they have to fill in.)

Quality control was aimed, says Houston, at restoring pride in the label "Clyde-built," a label which had been coming unstuck. It was to satisfy customers and, at the same time, safeguard the company's cash by eliminating the amount of abortive work. It also ensured that not too high a degree of expensive quality was achieved where it was unnecessary.

Coupled with this was *Value engineering* which reduced unnecessary costs built into specifications or production methods. One important aim of Value engineering was to agree a clause in a contract with a customer so that the yard and the customer, the shipowner, would divide between them any cash savings achieved by the acceptance of proposals submitted by the yard to change certain specifications on the ship under construction. On one occasion, the yard objected to the change suggested by an owner in the layout of the ship's dentist's chair. On closer investigation the owners discovered that there was in fact no need for the dentistry section on board at all, with consequent savings in room, equipment and the dentist's salary!

Operational research was a computer-assisted science which would enable the yard management to examine in detail the best way to lay out the whole work flow of the yard, the most lucrative type of ship they could quote for on world markets and the effect upon resources of men, money and machinery if certain enquiries were converted into orders. It would enable the yard to know how future work would fit in with existing commitments, so that they would know what promises they could or could not make. It would also allow them to state in exact terms of time and cash what the effects would be for any change in design or specification asked for by a client after an order had been taken. This system was worked on in conjunction with a Scottish university research unit.

Personnel management was also a department which came under the Productivity Services Director, for the employees were the most important asset and the most sensitive aspect of a company aiming to increase its efficiency.

Some indication has been given of the training necessary to ensure the efficient introduction of the Productivity Services, but it must be remembered that so far this was all directed towards improving the management control of the workers. It did not improve the skill of the workers nor did it lay down any foundations for a future skilled workforce.

Iain Stewart's message to industry was that insecurity meant fear and resentment; this led to resistance to new ideas for fear of unemployment which in turn created a situation where the unions defended overmanning, so that a job supported two or three workers instead of one. Stewart insisted, vehemently, that retraining was essential to remove fear of unemployment whilst at the same time reducing the number of workers required to carry out the work to be done. He was adamant that in many industries men had to be trained

120

to do two or three different kinds of work or that in a life-
time many workers would have to change their trades two
or three times. Industry is developing and changing so
rapidly, that one cannot at the start of a working life know
how long a particular trade is going to exist or in what
quantities work is going to be available for the workforce
in that trade.

In Sweden, Stewart pointed out, workers do not have any
fear of unemployment, do not need to try to hang on to
their jobs for years after the work has dried up, because there
are facilities for redundant men to be retrained into a trade
which needs labour. Their wages and social status are maintained during the retraining period and then, without loss
of revenue, they are qualified to plunge into a brand new
industry with new work prospects. The jealous defence of
jobs by unions in Britain and the rigid demarcation
principles, prevents men from moving from a defunct trade
into a booming one, and this spirit of dread and suspicion
has been bred by this constant fear of rotting away as an
unemployed man if a job is lost.

The new management also set out, therefore, to retrain
men into new trades and it succeeded in persuading unions
in the yard to abolish demarcation, achieving an open system
of flexibility and interchangeability.

"Well," relates Houston, "when this chap said to me, 'I
want to be a sheet iron worker all my life,' I said, 'OK,
then, go on, be an unemployed sheet iron worker.' "

Houston does not permit people to quote the Fairfields
management as being against demarcation completely. He
maintains:

> Not at all, we are all for some form of *demarca-
> tion*, but in management language we call it
> *specialisation*. We don't want the electricians to
> fix our plumbing and we don't want the welders to
> build our wooden decks. What we want is for an

electrician to be able to drill a simple hole when he's fixing up a lamp, just as any householder would be competent to do. When there's no work left for the sheet metal worker, we want to be able to train him as a plater or as a welder where there is a shortage of men. Why can't a man have two trades, so that he can be a steelworker when he's building the ship and then a painter when it needs finishing, instead of two lots of men doing a leap-frog through their lives of work, unemployment, work, unemployment? Then we could have twice as many men building the ship and twice as many painting it, finishing it in half the time with no one unemployed!

In very simple terms, those were the objectives inherent in the Fairfields policy.

Houston interpreted these policies to the yard men in his customarily forthright way: "It takes only four years to produce a Master of Arts at St Andrews University. Why the hell should it take five years to teach an apprentice how to be a bloody painter?"

He pointed out that, in fact, the honours graduate spent only 120 weeks at university, whereas a plumber's apprentice had to spend 250 weeks in a shipyard before he could be regarded as qualified. Of course, on investigation, it was shown that the apprentices received virtually no formal training at all. They were expected to hand the tools around and run errands and had to pick up their trade as best they could, very much dependent upon the plumber or welder they worked alongside.

Fairfields had to build a training centre (there were no training facilities to speak of in the yard previously) and PA Management Consultants were retained to set up a new apprentice training scheme. This was put under the control of a new man from outside, Gordon Mellis, who came in from Honeywell's, where he had trained men to build computers.

The Centre covered 7700 square feet (715 m²) and incorporated a seventy-seater lecture theatre equipped with the most up-to-date audio-visual aids. Twelve training supervisors were recruited from inside the yard and trained as instructors. Programmed learning techniques were employed to build up Craft Training Courses. A workshop training area was equipped with machinery to provide basic training in nine major trades which would apply to over 90 per cent of the work done in the yard. The remaining skills were taught on machines in the yard itself.

Before starting the training course, the apprentices were given health and eye tests and aptitude examinations to assess how well fitted each was for the trade he had chosen.

The great breakthrough was the acceptance of the unions to reduce the apprentice training period from five years to four years and the agreement for all apprentices to be trained in their first year, not for any specific trades, but as "shipyard workers." In this first year, before choosing their trade, they received a wide basic training in all crafts "in order to appreciate the problems of fellow craftsmen." They were given comprehensive instruction in the basic principles of work study, network analysis and quality control so that the future evaluation of trade work would be performed with those principles in mind. The new apprentices would be sufficiently skilled in such a wide range of jobs, that any future retraining to meet fluctuating work flow could be effected with the minimum amount of disruption. The final three years of his training brought the apprentice up to the best possible standards of his selected specialist trade.

The young workers were still under the supervision of a trained instructor when they moved out to work in production jobs in the yard and not left entirely to the mercy of their older fellow workers. The foremen, it was universally recognised, were too busy supervising work in progress to

123

serve at the same time as instructors of new boys. The modern equipment of the Training Centre was also flexible enough to be used in the further training or retraining of adult workers and for the examination of the standards of workers. In 1966 only forty applications were made for seventy apprenticeship vacancies, but, without any advertisement, over 750 applications were made in 1967. This was the change in the local families' confidence in the future of shipbuilding under the influence of the Fairfields system.

As Houston says, when they were not working they were teaching. Fairfields yard became a miniature university, where men and boys and management and researchers studied new ways of running a shipbuilding enterprise. In Stewart's first speech to the men, in December 1965 at the Lyceum, he had indicated that the yard would have to "pursue on a trial and error basis the application of new systematic techniques such as time study, work measurement, the handling of job cards, the recording of lost time, the payment of an upstanding wage and the commitment of all to make this joint enterprise profitable." "Trial and error" was a key phrase, for he could not expect to push through all these reforms without making mistakes.

Mistakes were made.

Four days after the Magna Carta of Fairfields, the Procedure Agreement, was signed midst national praise, when strikes and stoppages were banned for ever, the Boilermakers apprentices walked out!

They walked in again and out again five times between June and November, chalking up a total of 21 722 lost attendance hours. The dispute was the result of a verbal promise, made off the cuff by Oliver Blanford, who said during a negotiation on increased pay for productivity improvement by the Boilermakers members that the company would "look after the boys." The union shop stewards interpreted this as meaning that the Company would follow the normal custom of giving the apprentices a pro rata increase in pay based on the qualified workers' increases. The apprentices were told of this, but later the company maintained that their new Apprentices Charter with its improved training facilities and higher wages for age groups took the place of any previous system of increases. Both sides, the shop stewards and the management, took a stand on matters of principle. There were, it has to be said, probably also some matters of principle at stake between different members of the Fairfields management committee, where differences of personality had to shake down together in the early days. At the same time, there was also a measure of a trial of strength between management and the Boilermakers, with a very watchful band of other unions looking on.

The Boilermakers, employing almost 50 per cent of the yard workers, with the rest shared by twelve other unions, had always previously used their strength to assure favourable terms for its own membership. The new management had to show that it was able to "tame" the Boilermakers, then all the other wild elements would also agree to "come to heel." These are terms taken from the old atmosphere of negotiation, but they began to reappear during this first (and what proved to be the most critical) labour dispute that Fairfields had to face.

The Boilermakers shop stewards did however reveal a true spirit of co-operation, avoiding any use of a stoppage by the adult workers and promising the end to the walk-out in the Central Joint Council meetings. But the shop stewards were themselves embarrassed by the intransigence of the apprentices. The boys continued to lay down tools in spite of the promises made by Willy Duffy and Charlie Sim, two Boilermakers shop stewards, and Pat Kelly, their Clydeside Delegate, who continued to negotiate with the management through June, July and right up to December. The value of the CJC was proved in that the dispute was contained entirely as a matter of apprentices and did not spread. Finally, both sides, union and management, agreed to call Iain Stewart in as arbitrator to settle the matter. He had remained aloof, leaving it to the yard people to thrash it out, and when approached he refused to give any judgement. He stressed the gravity of the matter, insisting that the negotiating machinery they had established did not embrace independent arbitration. The CJC had to sink or swim on its own ability to resolve disputes.

Eventually a formula was reached which met some of the Boilermakers' apprentices' demands and saved management principles. The union agreed to accept that all apprentices were *shipyard* apprentices in the first year, belonging to no individual trade. All apprentices would therefore receive equal pay, not based on productivity bonuses, for they were not productive workers. However, certain of the older existing apprentices would be granted a *pro rata* increase as they had started their apprenticeship under different conditions. This agreement was a landmark in that it was the final recognition by everyone in the yard that apprentices were not just little, lesser-paid workers, but really students.

The Boilermakers did receive some favourable treatment (including an "advance" on productivity benefits in return for agreement to the productivity scheme) which riled other unions and prompted a spate of requests for increases and a one-day cranemen's strike. They argued that as the Boilermakers (who did all the steelwork) were producing more, then the cranesmen must be shifting more, in other words, being more productive. The management could not see how cranemen's work could be fitted into a new productivity scheme, but ended by offering a bonus in return for more flexibility—cranemen had to agree to move from one crane to any other which needed operating during the day instead of sticking to just the same machine the whole day, even when it was idle. This was considered an increase in productivity. During the crane drivers' strike the problem was highlighted of having a yard Convener who was also a shop steward for an individual section of the yard. Alex

126

McGuiness was the Convener who was supposed to take an overall dispassionate view between unions and yet he had to represent the cranemen who opposed favourable treatment for the Boilermakers. It must also be pointed out that the Boilermakers never accepted McGuinness as overall yard Convener, but kept to their own stewards. The management turned a blind eye to this, even allowing the Boilermakers' Convener to settle in a little office of his own "to make him less conspicuous."

It might have been better for the Company to have been firmer with its largest union but Iain Stewart defends management's action by claiming that a real showdown might have wrecked the tremendous atmosphere of goodwill which had been created at the start and any lengthy strike situation would have ruined the yard irrevocably at that point in time.

As it was, Fairfields strike record was still a tremendous improvement over previous years, even including the hours lost by the apprentices.

The number of hours of work lost through disputes between comparable periods of eleven months is:

Fairfield Shipbuilding and Engineering, 1964   41 264 hours
Fairfield Shipbuilding and Engineering, 1965   96 837 hours
Fairfields (Glasgow) Limited, 1966   24 746 hours

This was a reduction of 40 per cent compared with 1964, and a reduction of 74.4 per cent compared with 1965.

If adult working hours only are compared, then the improvement is as much as 92.6 per cent and 96.8 per cent.

Another mistake in the "trial and error" period of the yard's development was to pay so much attention to training shop stewards and gaining their co-operation, that the foremen and middle management felt neglected and became somewhat apathetic. The foremen were not able to see clearly what their own responsibilities were and what part they played in the new deal. This danger became apparent, in fact, from the first report produced by Kit Jenkins after a survey of attitudes and environment. There was some confusion concerning the overlap of responsibilities between foremen and shop stewards.

Oliver Blanford reports how wide was the variance between what management thought the foreman's job should be and what the foremen thought their job was. The foremen did not regard as their responsibility absence or lateness on the part of their men, they were not concerned about the costs of a job under their charge, they did not all consider it their duty to inspire leadership or team spirit nor to meet delivery dates. They had had no training in leadership or administration or in forward estimating, yet each foreman had between thirty and seventy men under his charge.

The new Fairfields management first gave some added status to the foremen by putting them on salaries instead of weekly wages. They then reduced team sizes down to fifteen on a ship and twenty-five in a workshop. Training sessions were instituted at weekend and week-long courses. It was also made clear that the foremen were the main line of communication down from the management. The shop stewards were spokesmen for the men only when it was a question of representing their interests in a dispute with foremen or management.

Section by section a completely new yard structure was built up, with each component part, each man, each group of men and each line of authority knowing their function, their responsibilities and their objectives. All the negotiations followed one after the other like frames on a speeded-up film, for new levels of productivity could not be achieved and profits could not be made until the systems were fully operational. At times productivity actually decreased and some graphs showed up worse. For a period there seemed to be a growing tendency for men to note down increased "waiting time," that is time in which they could not work because they were in need of materials or crane assistance or a foreman's advice or something. Critics of Fairfields (for everything was known to everyone, inside and outside the yard) said that the new management had very kindly given each worker twenty reasons why he might be allowed to stand idle and get paid for it! But Fairfields combated these remarks by pointing out that at least they became aware of any fault in a system within seven days or at most two weeks and could then rapidly find a solution. They did not have to wait a year for the balance sheet to indicate that something had been going wrong.

It took from January 1966 to June 1967 to prepare the way for the introduction of the Measured Daywork scheme, the culmination of the timing, observing, negotiating and debate. This scheme set down standards of output per hour for every job. Men were paid a basic rate for reaching a percentage of maximum efficiency. There were bonuses for any improvement on that target, worked on a group basis, with a squad of perhaps twelve men sharing the bonus they achieved jointly. This meant that a squad would work as a team, intent on producing maximum output. Each squad contained different kinds of tradesmen to complete a particular job from beginning to end, with drillers, caulkers and welders working in unison without problems of demarcation. There was no longer any need to hold up work constantly whilst an electrician foreman contacted a plumber foreman as in the old days. A squad was under the supervision of one foreman who was responsible for the speedy, economic completion of a whole section of a ship.

If a team were held up due to delay in providing them with the necessary work, materials or equipment, they were entitled to mark down "waiting time" which earned them their average pay. Weekly records were compiled and if an unacceptable level of "waiting time" was logged, then action was taken to rectify an obvious fault, by improving planning or repositioning machinery or educating the foreman, whatever was necessary. These records showed in detail how much work was achieved, at what cost (including time spent on spoilt or "abortive" work) and how it compared with the schedule if the ship were to be completed to the promised delivery date. Whenever a section of the work began to fall behind schedule, action could be taken well enough in advance to catch up. "As in a football match," explained Houston to the men, "when you know at half-time that you're one goal down, it does give you a chance of changing tactics and winning the game before the final whistle. It's when you don't even know the score in the game you're playing that you're in real trouble."

In the old Fairfields there had been a system of payment for work actually done, but it fell down on two important points. First, there were so few people capable of measuring the work done, that considerable amounts of time were wasted whilst the men waited for someone to come and measure their progress and give them something else to get on with. There were approximately only twenty men with the authority to measure the daily work of nearly 5000 employees.

Secondly, as the Head Timekeeper and Wages Clerk, Alec Hill, remembers, there would have been a severe crisis if any worker's wage fell below the average 9s 10d (£0.49) an hour, so wages had to be made up to that, anyway. Being operated in only a half-hearted manner, the old system simply added to overheads and delays without increasing productivity. The entire purpose of the new Measured Daywork system was to make sure that the men and the yard profited from a bigger output of good quality work for the hours put in. It was a partnership, with, as Oliver Blanford stressed, "management's job to provide the opportunity to earn a bonus through better planning and the men's job to work steadily, record non-productive time and abortive work and to earn £2 a week extra in bonus."

The men threw themselves into the "B for bonus" scheme with gusto, good humour and, on the serious side, the know-

130

ledge that without some such scheme to generate improved efficiency, there might be no jobs, certainly no wage rises, in the future. One way or another they had to catch up on the productivity gap which kept the Swedish and Japanese and German yards so far ahead of British shipbuilders. The time had come to stop the complaints, the excuses and the exhortations. The time had come to do that bit of extra work with that bit of extra efficiency which would make all the difference between bankruptcy and profits for all; profits for the Government, for the private and union shareholders and profits, too, in bonuses, for the yard workers.

George Gray, the Convener of the Boilermakers' shop stewards, found an anonymous ballad on a notice board which seemed to sum up the attitude of the men to the new rules.

> Twas B day down in Fairfields,
>   When the bonus scheme began;
> The men did not take time to walk,
>   In fact they almost ran.
>
> The foremen ran in circles,
>   To get every man a job;
> The men began to toil and sweat,
>   Their target was two bob.
>
> The boys in blue began to wonder,
>   If their times were tight;
> For if that proved to be the case,
>   We knew we'd have a fight.
>
> To try and show the working lads,
>   And make them understand;
> The estimated times they had,
>   Were fairest in the land.

The time and motion study men,
Went down upon the floor;
To see if any working lad
Would come and ask for more.

They soon had one or two requests,
To prove the times were tight;
And when they analysed results,
They found the times were right,

So forward into battle lads,
And hasten on the day,
When once again we show the rest,
We CAN make Fairfields pay.

Let's build the ships the modern way,
And we can say with pride;
The finest ships you'll ever see,
Are built upon the Clyde.

Needless to say, that ballad (which fits the tune of *Macnamara's Band*) was reproduced on the front page of the next issue of *Fairfield News*.

Chapter eight

The Urgent Merger

The Fairfields "proving ground" came to a premature end, just at the point when it was beginning to prove something.

Fairfields (Glasgow) Limited, under Iain Stewart and his motley Board, operated from January 1966 until February 1968, two short years crammed with excitement, drama and hectic activity and crowned with no mean achievement.

Strikes were drastically reduced, men's wages were increased through bonuses, orders for new ships were won in fair and open competition with the world, productivity increases were ten times greater than the national average that the Government called for. Six ships were built in that time, the three that were taken over in mid-construction were delivered more quickly than the owners had expected at the time of the bankruptcy announcement in October 1965; whilst the three ships built from beginning to end (or stern to bow under the new system) were kept strictly to the promised delivery programme, being handed over either exactly on time or ahead of time.

An outside management consultancy company, P-E Consulting Group Limited, commissioned at Stewart's request by the Upper Clyde Shipbuilders' Board, reported that Fairfields (Glasgow) Limited would show profits of £10 000 for the year 1967 (in two years, not three or five as Stewart

133

had promised Brown) and they forecast profits in 1968 of £296 000!

The yard was actually very disappointed at this report, for their own estimates had been £81 000 for 1967 and £782 000 for 1968. The Board still felt that these higher figures were realistic (there are many permutations of choice when making up a balance sheet) but always thereafter quoted only the figures provided by the independent investigation.

The quality of the yard's work was so high that Reardon Smith, the Cardiff shipping company which received two bulk carriers from Fairfields, praised their performance and promptly placed new orders for two further vessels.

One of the highlights of the yard's progress was the winning of orders for two US Navy survey ships, worth £6 million. Not only did Fairfields underbid competition for this contract, but the yard had to satisfy the US Navy that it could meet extremely stringent quality control requirements. Five American Naval advisers flew from the States and spent three days in the Govan yard in August 1966, interviewing management, inspecting facilities, talking with workers and examining the new systems being introduced. They liked what they saw and recommended Fairfields for the orders, which came through the same month. Roy Mason, Minister of State for Shipping, sent a telegram of congratulations to the yard.

In his paper "The Fairfields Project" published by University of Strathclyde in 1967, Jim Houston compared the number of manhours needed to fit out the inside machinery spaces on two identical ships, one built by the old Fairfield and one under the new management. These ships were *Atlantic City* (Job 831) and *Indian City* (Job 834), cargo liners for Reardon Smith Company. Both of these vessels were launched and completed by the new Fairfields, but *Atlantic City* had had its engine rooms fitted out prior to the takeover. *Indian City* was started from scratch by the new team.

Atlantic City's machinery spaces took the yard 29 weeks
to fit out, totalling 68 078 manhours. The comparable figures
for the identical sister ship, *Indian City*, were twenty-two
weeks for a total of 49 000 manhours. This was a saving of
19 078 manhours, showing 28 per cent increased efficiency.
(See page 142.) The average increase in efficiency to make
British industry really prosperous is estimated at 3 per cent.

The experts can argue a great deal about efficiency statistics,
and many have claimed that Fairfields certainly proved one
thing—that they were good at drawing graphs. However,
that independent report by P-E Consulting Group came to
the following conclusions:

> Between 1964 and June 1967 (covering the last
> two years of the old company and the measuring
> and studying period of the new firm) productivity
> dropped by 19 per cent.
>
> From June 1967 (when the measured daywork
> scheme was started) overall productivity increased
> by approximately 30 per cent.

The report compares Fairfield's position at January 1968
(exactly two years after the takeover) with the yard's performance four years previously, when it was at its most
efficient, immediately after the implementation of the previous
company's £5 million modernisation scheme. Stewart's
approach had produced enormous increases in productivity
with no significant investment in machinery but with un-
paralleled investment in training and work study. The P-E
report states:

> Percentages have been calculated to the same base
> and are thus directly comparable. The figures there-
> fore suggest an overall improvement of approxim-
> ately 10 per cent over 1964. In thus relating
> present performance to 1964 it should be noted

that, so far as steelwork is concerned, the old company's performance was then significantly better
than elsewhere on the Upper Clyde and compared
well with any yard in the UK.

It was of course still early days, only six months after the
introduction of the productivity payments scheme. The P-E
report comments:

> The major part of the potential for improving
> productivity is still to come. It was not possible in
> this survey to conduct the depth studies and exten-
> sive activity sampling necessary to make an objec-
> tive assessment of the remaining potential.
>
> The view was nevertheless formed and this view
> is shared by the Company, that productivity could
> be improved by a further 50 per cent or more.
>
> The necessary administrative and technical
> departments have been established to make these
> further gains and work is proceeding in many
> directions to secure them.

Blanford and Houston and their colleagues had created the
skeleton of a great new enterprise. It is a pity they were not
permitted to finish the job of building it up with flesh for
the future. Aspects of the new yard which were beyond
question were the spirit of leadership and the atmosphere
of hope and confidence which had been newly created. Wit-
nesses to that come from many quarters. The yard had a
constant stream of visitors representing every shade of outside opinion (with the exception of other Clyde shipbuilders). For the Labour Government there were George
Brown, Douglas Jay, Michael Stewart and many individual
MPs, including Emmanuel Shinwell. Special honour was
paid to George's wife, Sophie Brown, by inviting her to
perform the new organisation's first keel-laying ceremony

when the keel was set down for the £8 million guided missile destroyer HMS *Antrim* just two weeks after the Company was formed.

From the Conservative Opposition, yard visitors included the Leader, Ted Heath and the Opposition spokesman on labour affairs, Sir Keith Joseph. For several years Iain Stewart had maintained a parallel lobbying technique for his philosophy on industrial relations. During the Tory years he had badgered the Government and at the same time had been a frequent visitor to the home of Hugh Gaitskell, where he had also contacted George Brown and Ray Gunter in very early days. During the cash-hunting period when Stewart and Brown were trying to set Fairfields up, Stewart had made it his business to keep the Tory Opposition fully informed of the principles of the new enterprise to avoid any unnecessary political obstacles. On one occasion, in Room 509 at the Dorchester, Stewart was host to Ted Heath, Edward DuCann, Tony Barber and other leading Tories, quietly and judiciously briefing them on his plans and progress, when George Brown announced on the house phone that he was downstairs and about to come up. Stewart, to avoid a possibly very embarrassing confrontation, told Brown that he was a guest at a mixed party and could not therefore invite Brown up. George Brown was very suspicious, but in fact imagined that Stewart was having a secret meeting with Thomson behind his back, so he checked all round, only to discover that Roy Thomson was in Canada. He went away and, at eight o'clock the following morning, Stewart received a call from Brown who had rung to apologise for doubting his word.

Most of the leaders of the trade unions with members in shipbuilding journeyed to Fairfields to have a look round or sign agreements. University Professors popped in. Every major newspaper sent a top journalist to find a story and the yard inspired such disciples as Chris Brasher of *The Observer*, the late Harold Wincott of the *Financial Times* and Glyn Jones, BBC Producer and author of *Half-time Britain*. Many columnists from local Scottish papers practically lived there. Jack McGill of the *Scottish Daily Express* found his scepticism weakening more and more as Fairfields went on. He had brought off some gratifying scoops on the story in the early days, especially once when he was sitting inside Thomson House, phoning out stories which Bill Hawkins was forbidden to give to his own papers inside the building.

When Sean Connery accepted Iain Stewart's invitation to see for himself what was being done, he became so enthusiastic that he made the film *The Bowler and the Bunnet*, giving up six weeks of his time as a contribution to the project. He felt he had discovered at Fairfields that "esprit de corps" which he believes Scotland badly needs to counteract "the feudal atmosphere which still exists there."

An intriguing testimonial came from two young men who had gained a Centenary Scholarship from the Nottingham Chamber of Commerce. They were sixth form boys at a Nottingham school and they visited seven yards in Sweden and six in Scotland, including four on the Upper Clyde.

At the end of their project they wrote a report on their experiences, which is illuminating because it comes from two completely innocent lookers-on and is very forthright in its judgements. Of Stephen's yard, it said:

> As the first British shipyard to be visited, Stephen of Linthouse did not make a very good impression. We found that, despite the fact that the tour round the yard itself was perfectly satisfactory, some people with whom we spoke were not very interested in what we were doing and, in fact, tried to be rid of us as soon as possible.
>
> ... Stephen's employ over 3500 men in their yard, although, from general impressions during the visit, it would appear that little more than one

third actually work at any one time. This is due
partly to the demarcation problems introduced by
the unions and partly to the fact that the workers are
paid on time rate and can thus earn a good wage by
doing nothing. One cannot, however, assume that
the management is entirely blameless—incentive
and bonus schemes do not play such a large part at
this yard as at some other (in particular
Fairfields). . . .

The two seventeen-year-old youths, Marsh and Bownass, then
went over to John Brown's yard, and were delighted with the
hospitality shown them by the Managing Director, John
Rannie, but their fearless report said:

Brown's was a very old yard with a great deal
missing in the way of modern techniques. The men
seemed to work harder than at Stephens, but an air
of despondency was still prevalent.

Brown's have, in fact, six building berths, but at
the time of visiting only one was in use—that
holding the Queen Elizabeth 2 (Q4)—the only
berth in preparation for use was for the ore-carrier
which Brown's are building on their own initia-
tive. This they hope to sell once it is built. It seems
unfortunate to have only one berth in use at once,
particularly when orders would be available for the
others if it were not for the over-concentration of
effort on the Queen Elizabeth 2. The yard's skills
are based on the old established methods. When
questioned about the efficiency of slipway launching, the reply given was, "It has never failed yet, so
why should we change it." This is surely not a
maxim which should be heard, in one of the most
famous shipyards in the world. . . . It is interesting
to note that the shipbuilding side of John Brown

is entirely supported by the other interests of the company and that without these other firms, bankruptcy would be almost inevitable for the shipbuilding sector of John Brown, a great contrast to Kockums of Malmö [one of the Swedish yards the boys had already seen].

The boys also went to Yarrow's yard, which they noted had secured "one of the most lucrative sectors of the British ship-building industry, that of Naval construction." They pointed out that the Yarrow yard seemed modern and efficient, and was consistently profitable. However, they again reported on general atmosphere and spirit with the following passage:

> Our reception at Yarrow was very cordial but it appeared that the Personnel Officer was going to "pass the buck" with respect to our visit. This fear was justified and we were taken off to the Training Department, where the unsuspecting Training Officer was given the task of arranging our visit. He appeared to be a very busy man and whilst waiting for our tour to begin we spoke to one of the older members of the Training Department. We pointed out the fact that many of the men seemed dreadfully inactive and were doing nothing most of the time. He became quite irate and said that the younger generation were to blame because they were so lazy. We did not agree and tried to show that the example of the older men would improve the attitude of the younger people. This general attitude that the other person was always to blame was very widespread and until it is altered it becomes a major problem of the British shipbuilding industry.

Perhaps the next time the Government sets up any Commission or Committe of Inquiry, it would be advised to number amongst the members a couple of astute, keen sixth formers. It is amazing what they were able to record in Sweden and Scotland working on a total grant of £100. Their comments on Fairfields went right to the heart of the experiment. It was typical of Fairfields that the man given the duty of conducting their tour round the yard was a union official, Alex McGuinness the Convener of Shop Stewards. After the tour, the boys wrote:

> Fairfields employ professional management and work on a basis of measured productivity. This new Measured Daywork scheme employs men to their best ability and output. Fairfields are also encouraging and promoting retraining schemes for men who might be laid off because of fluctuations in labour requirements due to changes in demand for a certain product. This policy of retraining is one which has been usefully borrowed from Sweden where never less than 1 per cent of the working population are participating in retraining schemes at any one time... Fairfields future is, in their own opinion, good. They are convinced that, given the chance now they can make good all the errors of the past. From the general impression which we obtained we would agree and think that it is a pity that Fairfields may never get the chance to show themselves as being a valid independent concern because of the proposed merger of the five main shipyards on the Upper Reaches of the Clyde, a good idea perhaps unfortunate in its timing for Fairfields.

This sentiment was the final paragraph in so many reports, articles and speeches of the time. In February 1968 Harold

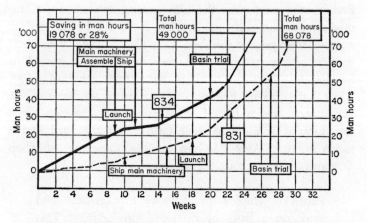

3 FITTING-OUT ENGINE ROOMS ON *Atlantic City* (831) AND *Indian City* (834)

Wincott ended a major feature article in the *Financial Times* on the Fairfields experiment with the words: "But one does fear that the verdict on the Fairfields experiment will be: 'If only we had had another two years.' It deserves a better epitaph than that."

Fairfields (Glasgow) Limited had been brought into being against all the odds by a combination of lucky circumstances. Iain Stewart, the industrial philosopher, found a proving ground right next door to his office at Govan; he had a friend and financial adviser, Derek Palmar, who was an inside man at the Department of Economic Affairs; and there was a Government Minister, George Brown, willing and able to charge through any obstacles in their path.

But Fairfields was born to die. Its end was foreshadowed in its very creation, for George Brown had to promise his Cabinet colleagues, the Opposition, the Confederation of British Industry and the Shipbuilders' Employers' Federation that Fairfields would not stand in the way of any Clyde mergers necessary for the future health of the industry as a whole. The Fairfields yard was going to be saved only in order to be able to hand it over, alive, to whatever was

142

thought best by the Geddes Shipbuilding Inquiry Committee.

The Geddes Committee Report was published in March, 1966, less than three months after Fairfields (Glasgow) Limited was officially formed. Two short years from that, Iain Stewart had retired, hurt, back to his Thermotank office in Govan, Oliver Blanford had gone with a golden handshake, and Jim Houston had resigned. Fairfields was left as just one Division of five in the new Upper Clyde Shipbuilders group, whose Board was controlled by a majority of Directors from John Brown's, Stephen's, Connell's and Yarrow's. Stewart had won his battle for co-operation with the men and the unions, but had lost in the power game played by five managements. Probably his only saviour might have been a vigorous, unorthodox Cabinet Minister devoted to what Fairfields stood for in the future and had achieved in its brief past, but a lot had also happened to George Brown in those two years. He had resigned from the DEA, stayed with the Cabinet when offered the coveted job of Foreign Minister and then forfeited all Government power by resigning once again and moving to the back-benches. He was only a spectator when the merger moves were at their height. The Government shares had also had a chequered career. Organised by the DEA, the shareholding was nevertheless taken up officially by the Board of Trade. A little later, when responsibility for shipping and ship-building was given to the Ministry of Technology, Frank Cousins, the Mintech Minister and a sympathiser with Stewart's intentions, had the shares handed over to him. But, in that same eventful period of Harold Wilson's manoeuvres to drag Britain into the twentieth century, Cousins joined in the "kicking and screaming" and resigned from office and then from his seat in the House. Anthony Wedgwood Benn became Minister of Technology, holding the Fairfields shares which were by now little more than bric-à-brac found in the former Minister's cupboard. They were already dusty relics, compared with the brave new shipbuilding world he was introducing with his Shipbuilding Industries Bill. This followed the Geddes Report more faithfully and wholeheartedly than probably any Government action on any other Committee Report. Geddes urged mergers. The Report stated:

> We have found it necessary to envisage the grouping of yards into bigger enterprises as the only way in which the human and other resources needed for successful and competitive shipbuilding can be supported and kept in employment.

The Report maintained that it was essential to have new shipbuilding groups consisting of group headquarters with a number of yards specialised in different types of constructions. Within a group individual yards should concentrate on sophisticated ships (destroyers, frigates, passenger ships and large ferries) or multi-decked cargo ships or on bulk carriers and tankers. The first type would require extensive fitting-out operations and complicated hull construction and instrument installation. The second type demanded fairly complex steel work and hull construction, but much reduced fitting out, whereas the third type, the tankers, were simply vast metal containers, suitable for large-scale but simple production. This arrangement would enable a group to quote competitively on world markets because the best techniques and equipment could be set up within each specialised field. The days of scrambling for any type of order just to keep men employed and yards alive would be over.

The Clyde would divide logically into the Upper and Lower Reaches (two distinct arms of the river several miles apart), but rationalisation would not provide for more than one group for each. The Upper Clyde would have facilities for building the first two categories of ship (sophisticated naval and passenger ships and multi-deck merchant vessels and large ferries) but, because of the limitations of the river conditions, would not be able to cope with tankers above 100 000 tons (previously considered "giants" but then already dwarfed by 250 000 tonners under construction or planned elsewhere).

Between the setting up of Fairfields and the appearance of the Geddes Report, there was only time to squeeze in a couple of paragraphs relating to the new experiment. These were paragraphs 334 and 335:

> As is well known, the State took shares in Fairfield's partly because a loan could not keep this yard going while the future of the industry as a whole was under consideration, and partly because this enabled an experiment in industrial relations to be undertaken. The yard was, however, to be run on a commercial basis, and, although our investigations were not sufficiently advanced at the time the decision was taken to allow us to indicate how this particular yard might best contribute to the industry's competitiveness, we thought it possible that participation in a Clyde group might prove the right use of Fairfield's labour force and other assets. We accordingly sought and received confirmation that our freedom to make recommendations about the industry was not affected, that the Government would not undertake commitments or authorise long-term plans which would make it difficult for Fairfield's to be included in some structural reorganisation of the industry, and that the Fairfield-Rowan engine works would not be assisted to continue in main engine production on the assumption that we could suggest an assured role for it.
>
> Any one with the interests of British shipbuilding at heart will wish the Fairfield's experiment well and we should expect employers'

associations, like trade unions, to keep in touch with developments at this yard as well as other yards. At the same time we think that the future of Fairfield's may need early consideration. Other yards are also reaching new agreements and one of the problems to be faced by the new groups will be to reconcile the pay, working conditions and procedures in the various yards of the group. The early reconciliation of those at Fairfield's with those in other yards may not be easy and yet, if one or more groups were to form on the Clyde and reorganise without Fairfield's being included, the prospects of this yard or the balance of a group might be adversely affected.

The Government had committed itself to promising Geddes that the rescue of Fairfields would not jeopardise the success of any new grouping on the Clyde. The Fairfield-Rowan main engine side of the old Fairfield company had not been saved. It had been obvious the building of main engines in small manufacturing units all over Britain was no longer economic. Stewart did not want it inside his experiment. Brown and the Fairfield-Rowan Shop Steward Convener, Alex Jamieson, had fought hard to find a solution, but the engineering shops had been closed and the jobs lost.

Nothing the Government and Fairfields had done was contrary to the promise made to Geddes, or prejudicial to the interests of British shipbuilding as a whole.

Stewart and his Fairfields Board appreciated that there were very weighty reasons for putting Fairfields into an Upper Clyde merger. These were:

1   The promises made to Geddes and everyone else.
2   A later investigation which showed that Fairfield's facilities were vital to the viability of the region's shipbuilding efficiency as a whole. If Fairfields

stayed out, it might jeopardise the jobs of over 10 000 men in the future.

3   A merger was urgently required to go through smoothly, for at least two of the other yards would be unable to carry on without the financial assistance from the Government which was conditional upon the merger taking place.

4   The hope that Fairfield's new management systems and worker co-operation might be spread to five yards instead of restricted to one (a step to Stewart's dream of implementing his ideas nationally).

5   The clear-cut reminder from the Government, that financial pressure could very easily be brought to bear upon Fairfield's future if the yard did not come to heel.

It has to be remembered that the £1 million share capital had been used to purchase the Fairfield assets from the Receiver. The new company's working capital was supplied by Government loans at 7 per cent interest. Just under £1 million had been taken up by Fairfields (Glasgow) Limited and there were facilities for a further borrowing of half a million under certain circumstances (not to finance running losses but to provide for development if the new firm was proving itself viable). Derek Palmar, the Government's liaison Director, had to indicate to the Board that the new Minister-in-charge, Wedgwood Benn, would block any efforts to call on this additional sum if it were to be used to keep Fairfields going as an independent yard, scornful of the proposed merger.

Furthermore, the Geddes proposals made it difficult for independent yards to obtain other financial benefits, if it were thought that they should be merged. Credit facilities, expansion and reorganisation grants, cash for research by consultants, were all to be made available for the good boys.

If Fairfields was dubbed a "naughty boy," there would be precious little spending money to help it on its way.

Lashings of money were earmarked for the newly formed shipyard groups by Wedgwood Benn, far more even than that proposed by Geddes. Whereas Geddes suggested about £30 million of Government low-interest credit facilities for British shipowners buying from UK yards, Wedgwood Benn raised this figure to £200 million!

A substantial £20 million was placed in a box ready for the financing of new facilities in the yards and £5 million to cover "transitional losses," the cost of the wedding when yards got married.

These sums made British yards sit up and take notice. In 1966, the year that Geddes published the Report, the twelve shipyards which published accounts showed losses between them of £2.6 million. When the recommendations appeared, there were six yards operating on the Upper Clyde. By the time of the merger two years later, one had already dropped by the wayside, Barclay Curle, a subsidiary of the Tyneside company Swan Hunter. Only Yarrow's was making consistent profits in that area and they relied primarily upon naval orders. John Brown's, the biggest Clyde yard, for years had been entirely dependent upon its parent engineering group for subsidising its losses, Stephen's yard was running out of resources and Connell's was up and down, leaning on family investment when it was down. Fairfield's first annual balance sheet under Stewart showed later that up to 31 December 1966 the Company provided for trading losses of £220 000 and eventual losses on contracts in hand of a further £368 000.

Throughout Britain there was a sudden urge to merge when the yards read of the bounty which the Ministry of Technology was prepared to distribute.

The instrument recommended by Geddes for doling out the cash was a Shipbuilding Industry Board, which would "be enabled to make loans aimed at facilitating desirable groupings and accelerating the rationalisation of resources." The SIB would also act as a prime mover, cracking the whip, exhorting, twisting arms and supervising the formation of viable new groups. In the words of the Report, the SIB "would initiate, assist and stimulate necessary action within the industry; administer and control Government financial assistance; and give the Government informed advice on the current prospects of British firms and on the effect on their businesses of assistance given to shipbuilders overseas.'

The Government followed these recommendations exactly, although it took twelve months for the SIB to be established through proper legislation in the House of Commons. The proposal suggested "an independent chairman with experience of the problems of large industrial organisations" and the Government appointed William Swallow (now Sir William), former chairman of Vauxhall Motors, to head their SIB. His two colleagues on the new Board were Joe Gormley, Secretary of the North Western Area of the National Union of Mineworkers, and Anthony Hepper, seconded to the DEA from the Tilling Group of Companies, where he had been Managing Director of Pretty Polly, the successful stockings manufacturers.

The Clyde yards were quick off the mark when the Geddes proposals were published. On 22 August 1966, Yarrow's, Stephen's and Connell's, three family-run yards, announced plans to form a merger. They stated that the decision was the result of almost six months of negotiations. It was almost six months since the Geddes Committee had announced its recommendations.

This merger plan was a matter of concern to John Brown's and Fairfields. For years Lord Aberconway, Chairman of the John Brown parent group, had commented in his annual statements that he would be quite happy to be divested of the shipbuilding liability. The yard could hardly be expected to survive after the handing over of the QE2 to Cunard's.

The bulk carrier, the only other ship under construction in the John Brown (Clydebank) yard when those Nottingham schoolboys had visited it, was being built on spec, in the hope that some kind owner would come forward and buy it, almost certainly at a loss for the yard, when it was complete. The labour force dreaded the day when the QE2 (or Q4 as she was known then) would be handed over, for it would certainly mean unemployment for several thousand men. It was in the interests of the workers, who were paid for the time they worked, to keep the job going as long as possible. If his personal story comes to be told, we may learn one day what it would be like for the Managing Director, John Rannie, to be faced with the dilemma of meeting a delivery date and so bringing about the closure of the yard of which he was so proud. Which loyalty would be the greater?

Consequently, two weeks before the other three yards announced their definite decision to merge, the papers had carried the headlines that Brown's and Fairfields were to start merger talks. The main negotiations for this two-yard amalgamation took place in London. Oliver Blanford, Professor Alexander and Derek Palmar represented Fairfields. John Rannie led a three-man negotiating team for John Brown's. His colleagues were James Smyth, the parent group's Chief Accountant, and M O Hughes of Wallace Attwood, management consultants. Iain Stewart had corresponded at length with Lord Aberconway, who was anxious to marry his yard off to cut the losses.

But the negotiations were very sticky. Although the discussion was amicable, it was like trying to merge three members of a pop group with three from a "Palm Court" orchestra. Their tempos were out of step, especially when it came to a discussion of new management techniques. For example, a report from the Fairfields delegation stated:

> John Rannie argued that the general trend in shipbuilding is away from work study, which has been

150

tried extensively and found impracticable or un-
satisfactory. John Rannie explained that his own
system of work study, based on graded rates, had
been put up to the Geddes Committee and found
favour there. Unfortunately, the Unions opposed
the system, but there were still hopes of getting
away with it. John Rannie argued that with the
Cunarder on his hands he could not risk the upset
and interference which would be involved in the
introduction of work study. ("Anyway, where
could I get the staff?") He could not at this stage
advise his Board to use methods different from
those at present in use on the Q4 and would favour
the two yards being merged "in isolation." John
Rannie made it clear that he was not opposed to
work measurement in principle, but was opposed
to it in the short term on practical grounds. In any
event he wanted to stress that his time was coming
to an end and that he would not stand in the way
of new methods.

When he talks of his yard, the word "proud" comes into
John Rannie's vocabulary a lot. He has a personality in
keeping with the giant liner he built, but it is probably a
typical tragedy (for British industry if not also for Rannie
personally) that he was given the task of running the
Clyde's biggest yard and supervising every detail of the construction of one of the world's most complex ships, with
such little exposure to modern management techniques. He
was not even able to afford a quality control inspector in
the pipeshop department. As he says himself, over the 100
years of its existence, the Clydebank yard had grown "like
Topsy." The only solution would have been to build a completely new yard from scratch and the capital was not available.

At that point in time, John Brown's would not agree to
anything which smacked of a takeover. Any co-operation had

to be in the form of an equal merging of interests, and
Rannie was thinking in terms of keeping the yards isolated
from each other. Lord Aberconway would have to insist on
a joint Board for the new grouping. Stewart, however, could
not envisage a situation in which his executives would have
to be content to watch any old methods continuing when
the whole point of the exercise for Fairfields was an exten-
sion of their new methods. The QE2 was just the juicy
bone of contention Stewart would like to get his teeth into,
so that productivity improvements could once again be
forcibly brought to the attention of British industry as a
whole. For Stewart and Blanford and Houston to sit on a
joint Board which allowed Britain's most famous ship to be
built on the old hit and miss method was totally unacceptable.
Only another crash programme of planning and measurement
and control, on an even bigger scale than Fairfields, could
possibly hope to avoid a major Clyde disaster to mark the
sailing away of Britain's wonder ship. (This line of thought
had no connection with the unfortunate turbine troubles the
ship suffered, which were simply an added complication. The
turbines were constructed by John Brown Engineering, which
was not included in any merger talks, but which continued
as a separate turbine manufacturing company. Its main interests are now in the construction of advanced turbines for
non-marine applications. Fairfields' fears at that juncture
would be more related to the liner's later boiler-feed troubles
and the incomplete state of almost 100 cabins when the ship
was to be handed over.)

Stewart appreciated at that time that it would be an
economic step to take over Brown's and give that yard the
Houston treatment, because a quarter of a million pounds
had been invested in productivity services by Fairfields in
its first year. The enormous team of industrial engineers,
work study specialists and trained foremen, in Houston's
own words, "could now serve a yard four or five times bigger
than Fairfields." He had had to create that mighty produc-

tivity sledge-hammer to crack the Fairfields nut as an emergency operation. It could easily be swung in the direction of any other nearby nut, or nuts.

The negotiations continued between the two yards, but there were obviously going to be no satisfactory terms of merging, when a new factor turned up and threw all the Clyde plans back into the melting pot. Tony Hepper arrived on Clydeside with his Working Party from the Shipbuilding Industry Board.

Hepper headed a three-man delegation from William Swallow's newly formed SIB. His two colleagues were A W Giles, Managing Director of Baring Brothers, the merchant bankers, and J H F Macmichael, a director of P-E Consulting Group, the management consultants. Hepper's Working Party had the following terms of reference:

> To co-ordinate arrangements for the study and valuation of shipbuilding assets and facilities on the Upper Clyde and to make proposals for the formation of a group, for the consideration of the firms concerned in accordance with the recommendations of the Geddes Report. The working Party should also bear in mind the possibility of such a group being extended in due course to cover the whole of the Clyde and in the meantime should liaise with the proposed group on the lower Clyde.

The working Party was at that time welcomed by all five yards concerned on the Upper Clyde. The three family yards which had already announced merger plans wanted to qualify for the financial assistance from the SIBs funds. Of these, Yarrow (Shipbuilders) Limited employed 2000 men and would be the dominant partner as it was a profitable company concentrating on work for the Admiralty. Alexander Stephen and Sons Limited had been making big losses but had also about 2000 workers. Founded in 1750, it was one of Britain's oldest yards and was building mainly refrigerated cargo ships and dredgers, although its order book had run very thin. The Stephen family would not be able to subsidise it much longer. Charles Connell and Company (Shipbuilders) Limited was the smallest yard, with only 1000 men. It was run by a father and son, both called Charles Connell. The business had been founded in 1861 and had been predominant in building fast cargo liners.

John Brown's and Fairfields were two yards that none of the others wanted to merge with! John Brown's had 5000 men and a recent history of losses to daunt the others. Fairfields was the rogue yard. The shipbuilding families would not be willing to become involved unless they had the upper hand. Fairfields' estimate of the situation was that John Brown's would go out of existence, and the three-yard merger would then be in a position to swallow Fairfields with Government assistance.

Under the terms of Geddes, the intentions of the SIB and the promises made at the birth of Fairfields, a merger was inevitable. But Stewart preferred to eat rather than be eaten. A two-sided, three-sided and five-sided all-in wrestling match was on. Hepper and his men were on the spot as the judges and timekeepers. The real referee was Wedgwood Benn, looking distantly on from his Ministry watchtower on the Thames. Whenever there was an appeal for foul from the Clyde, Wedgwood Benn refused to become involved. Oliver Blanford tried in vain to get a hearing from him, John Rankin, the MP for Govan failed to move him to take action and Andrew Cunningham, Director of Fairfields and a Trade Union spokesman, complained to him in writing "that Labour Ministers are extremely difficult to talk to."

The problem is that the Government may well have played the whole game too fairly. They were more keen to let justice be seen to be done than to achieve real justice for the

British economy. There are times when management consultants' reports on production facilities and accountants'
reports on shareholding manipulations and settlements, and
bankers' reports on future working capital requirements and
profitability studies may all fall down for a lack of a deep
understanding of the personalities involved. What was
probably needed at that time on the Clyde more than anything else was a psychological survey of the attitudes of the
labour force and of the type of approach which would gain
the co-operation of the labour force. Without the men, the
management and the money are useless.

The merger terms which came into being were a generous
distribution of cash to the participating firms, seats on the
main Board for all the five yards and an impartial umpire,
Tony Hepper, as Chairman and Managing Director. It was
a Whitehall masterpiece of compromise, trying to please
everybody, with no one taking a firm view of what would
be the best for the Clyde, even if it were unpalatable to any or
all of the top people of the yards. Faces were saved all
round, speeches made about how each glorious yard would
add to the glorious future of the new grouping, but a Board
was constituted which could not possibly give any hope of
dynamic new action to the 13 000 workers it now controlled.
The unions had objected to Stewart when he had allowed
one former director of Fairfield Shipbuilding to come on to
the Board of Fairfields (Glasgow). Now all the yards were
to come under the control of a Board which included a
mixture of old yard managements and new people from
outside, with a Chief Executive, who had no experience in
leading men on the Clyde, and with the John Brown, Yarrow,
Stephen and Connell Directors holding a majority vote
together. Fairfields' ideas on how to run a shipbuilding
enterprise, the whole of the impetus of the Fairfields project,
were at the mercy of a combined vote of its former enemies.
But, to the Whitehall observers, it was a neat arrangement
of each yard having one vote. Conflicts of ideas, differences

of personalities were not taken into account either way. No one made a decision that Fairfields had been right or wrong and that the new group should be seen to be following that road or turning in another direction. The merger was formed to march steadfastly ahead, up each of the different roads indicated by the Board members.

When the merger terms had finally been agreed and the new Upper Clyde Shipbuilding group formed, there was a celebratory dinner at a Glasgow hotel. There were many speeches. Sir Charles Connell of Connell's yard, now a Director of UCS, stood up and remarked with a smile at Iain Stewart: "I must congratulate SIB on getting all the sheep into the pen, including the black one."

Iain Stewart made no merry speech of welcome. When urged to speak, he simply replied to Connell, "All the assets and the liabilities are neatly in the pen, but not the labour force." Stewart had never felt that his Fairfields venture was ready for congratulations the moment he had bought its assets from the Receiver!

Tony Hepper's Working Party arrived on the Clyde in April 1967 and produced a report by July 1967. Production and management studies were provided by combined teams from P-E Consulting Group and PA Management Consultants. Great attention was given to the vital need for increasing productivity to gain full benefit from the labour force and from the capital invested in equipment. The reports stated that in the context of large gains in productivity:

> ... the development of the Fairfields "experiment" will be viewed with great interest particularly with regard to its success or otherwise in achieving and sustaining a very large increase in productivity across the whole labour force in a very short space of time.
>
> If the attempt is fully successful Fairfield will have performed a great service on the Group's be-

half and their type of approach will no doubt rapidly be developed throughout. Even if the experiment falls short of attaining its full objectives it will no doubt provide valuable lessons and the means of accelerating progress.

Charles Connell and Company commented back on this:

Fairfield's Experiment can only be judged after orders which the new organisation obtained themselves are completed. The increases in productivity since the measured daywork scheme came in may only be returning productivity to the old level.

The tragedy for Stewart was that the Working Party report could only survey the eighteen months of the new Fairfields which had been devoted to investing in work measurement and productivity preparations. The Measured Daywork scheme only came into being in June 1967 and it is true that at that point there had been no time for an order to be obtained and built and delivered under the new management. The only aspect of the success which was not pure conjecture for the future was the new spirit of co-operation amongst the unions and men, which could not yet be measured in terms of profits.

The Working Party report recommended that the five yards should merge and that the facilities should be rationalised by phasing out Connell's and Stephen's yards. There were to be hull production divisions at Brown's and Fairfields and a specialised out-fitting division to serve the group. Yarrow's yard would continue to concentrate on naval ships.

There were three main conditions for the success of the merger. These were that all five yards had to agree to the terms; that the SIB provided the necessary finance to make the merger and re-organisation possible; and that a satisfactory Employment Charter could be negotiated with the unions. An important aspect of the Working Party's recommendations was the reduction of the overall labour force from about 13 000 to 7500! There had to be drastic "streamlining" in order to make the UCS group viable in the future.

The constituent yards were brought into the merger in the following way:

John Brown's received 30 per cent of the shareholding in the new group in return for its assets. This was highly satisfactory because it relieved the former parent firm of a continual drain and gave it a substantial part of a very much bigger enterprise well supported with Government funds.

Stephen's received 10 per cent of the shareholding in return for its assets, again a swap of a loss-maker for a share in the new group.

Yarrow's remained a separate company, Yarrow (Shipbuilders) Limited, but the new UCS group bought 51 per cent of its shares for £1 million. This was for the "amortised loss of profits," because Yarrow's would have been earning over £400 000 profits per annum and would not expect any dividends from the UCS group for some years. This meant, however, that the Yarrow shareholders still would own half (49 per cent) of their yard's profits and would benefit from the finance to be granted by SIB for expanding and modernising its facilities. The £1 million compensation, therefore, represented about half of the profits of the yard for a period of five years, paid in advance, for the privilege of making it a subsidiary. Yarrow's were allocated 20 per cent of the UCS equity.

Connell's received 200 000 of the UCS £1 shares, giving them a 5 per cent holding. In addition the company was paid £400 000 for profit on contracts which Connell's had negotiated to an advanced stage. Furthermore, Connell's were guaranteed a commission on future orders obtained by the UCS group from a specified long list of potential customers, which would be counted as arising from the goodwill created by Connell's in former business contacts. This commission could amount to several hundred thousand pounds.

Stewart was not present at the UCS meeting which agreed that arrangement with Connell's and, although he objected strongly at later meetings, he was powerless to amend it. He claimed that several of the shipowners on the list were contacts, too, of Fairfields and other yards and could not possibly be claimed exclusively by Connell's. He managed to get his objections minuted and, in vain, suggested an amendment to the Connell arrangement—this was that a commission of this magnitude should not be paid to Connell's until the group became profitable. This suggestion was rejected by UCS and it became a strong bone of contention with all the members of the Fairfields Board.

Fairfields received the biggest single shareholding in UCS, 35 per cent (reduced later to 32.5 per cent when some rights issues were not taken up by some Fairfields shareholders and were bought by John Brown's).

This was in respect of the valuable new equipment in the yard and the ship orders in hand which were greater than at any other yard. The Fairfields shareholders received £350 000 "in respect of expenditure on improving productivity and the discounted contribution to the future profits expected to arise from the productivity improvements. If the productivity improvements are realised there will be a benefit to the new company (UCS) of an amount greater than the cash payment." Those were the words of the management consultants' recommendation. This payment to Fairfields confirmed officially that the yard had become viable only eighteen months after the new management had taken over, because, in all, the shareholders received 1.3 million £1 share in UCS and £0.35 million in cash, which was altogether worth 66 per cent more than they had invested. However, Roy Thomson and Harold Salvesen indicated their wish to dispose of what remained of their original investment. They had supported the Government's proving ground and had no wish to invest in a completely new style of company, UCS. To insist on an immediate cash payment would have meant further delays, and so the transfer into UCS shares was completed in the belief that the machinery for withdrawal would come into operation after the merger was completed. But Wedgwood Benn did not feel it advisable for the Government to purchase UCS shares off them at that stage, desiring to leave the way open for others to do this. No one else has shown any interest in buying the shares and meanwhile, just over one year later, the shares have lost a considerable amount of their nominal value.

Negotiations are still going on about means of allowing Thomson and Salvesen to pull out, but have become bogged down in an interpretation of the SIB powers. These, as stated in Section 6 of the Shipbuilding Act, allow SIB to acquire *new* shipbuilding shares and, in Section 4, allow the SIB to make loans for the acquisition of existing shipbuilding shares in connection with a grouping scheme. According to the Minister of Technology, the former Fairfields shareholders fall between these two stipulations. The debate now raging is, "When are shipbuilding shares *new* and how long does it take for them to be termed *old*."

One of the potential tragedies in the share situation, judging from the financial straits of UCS, is that the first real move on the part of British trade unions to become investment partners in such a scheme as Fairfields looks like teaching them a lesson never to become involved again. It would be difficult for George Brown to talk unions into providing financial help in this way with such a precedent as a model.

There had been another yard, Barclay Curle's, on the north bank of the Clyde, just across from Stephen's and Fairfields. This was a subsidiary of the Tyneside shipbuilding firm of Swan Hunter. Early in 1967, it was announced that the yard could no longer be maintained and was available for sale. Swan Hunter approached Sir William Swallow of SIB and asked if his Board could find any means of ensuring continuity of employment for the workers there. Fairfields came into the picture at the end of February 1967, for they felt they could make profitable use of the berths at Barclay Curle's. The Barclay Curle yard, however, fell between two stools. It could not be saved because there was no one willing to take the authority to move one of the stools a little to support it.

Stewart was convinced that if he had the extra facilities at the threatened yard, he could obtain orders (especially for container ships) to make it viable. He also knew, from meetings held many months earlier, that there were a number of Scottish private investors quite keen to put some capital into Fairfields for expansion as soon as the way ahead was clear. Fairfields' one-year record of progress had impressed them, but Geddes made the future of Fairfields very unclear. Who would put cash into the enterprise when they did not know what was to become of the firm during the merger talks?

Sir William wrote to Stewart and assured him that the SIB was very "anxious that the facilities in the Barclay Curle yard should be preserved for shipbuilding until their usefulness to a possible Upper Clyde group can be examined." Swallow wrote: "The Board (SIB) are continuing to devote much effort to trying to achieve this."

So Stewart asked the SIB to devote less effort and more money, for it was simply a question of cash. A loan from SIB could bridge the gap, with Fairfields acting as caretakers of the Barclay Curle yard until the SIB Working Party had had time to consider how it would fit into the new grouping. Then, if it were found that Fairfields was to continue as a viable separate enterprise, it could raise the cash privately to purchase the yard. If however the Upper Clyde group was to come into being, incorporating all the local yards, then the new group could officially borrow the money from SIB to absorb the threatened yard. Swallow, however, made it clear once again that this "bridging" operation was not within the terms of reference of SIB, so Barclay Curle's went out of existence and its site is now being offered as an industrial development plot.

There was no Government Minister who felt sufficiently personally involved and sufficiently personally powerful, to take some speedy action to keep that yard and its jobs alive just a few weeks longer. Stewart felt bitter at the loss of such a conveniently placed extra shipbuilding berth which he was certain Fairfields could have kept in work if the imminent mergers had not cast such a shadow over the future.

The Fairfields Board realised that there was little chance of escaping from a merger. What occupied them (for several months) was the *method* of merging. They could see a great chance of disaster for their experiment if the yards were to merge on any basis of "equality," for that sort of equality would, of course, put Fairfields in a minority of one yard against four. They desperately wanted the experiment to survive, at least long enough to prove itself more conclusively so that it could stand as a model for other branches of industry. Although the Board was entirely committed to making the Fairfield yard profitable, all its members were there to carry out an investigation into the effects of Stewart's philosophy applied to a real industrial unit.

Palmar was watching it for the Department of Economic Affairs and the Ministry of Technology, the official mid-wives to Britain's industrial re-birth. Lord Carron and Andrew Cunningham were ready to spread the gospel throughout the Trade Union movement if it was shown to work. Professor Alexander was documenting every move and reaction in human terms at every level in the yard for widespread study in economics and academic circles. Sir Jack Scamp might use his observations at Fairfields to good effect when called in to settle labour disputes in other industries, at which he was a nationally recognised expert. Oliver Blanford and Jim Houston were already lecturing up and down the country on every detail of their work-in-progress. Chapters were being written all the time on the Fairfield adventure. It was an engrossing serial story and there would be severe disappointment if there were to be an inconclusive ending.

Stewart had spent years trying to make a start to his new industrial revolution. Fairfields was for him the platform from which to step to much bigger applications of his philosophy as an answer to Britain's industrial problems. There were many policies still to be tried. For Iain Stewart the word "security" for workers did not mean continuity of employment in any specific job. It meant transferable pensions, continuity of income and continuity of established living standards, which could only be achieved by retraining for expanding trades any workers who became unemployed in a shrinking trade. At Fairfields they retrained 13.8 per cent of the labour force in less than two years, whilst the Scottish average was 0.1 per cent and the national British average 0.06 per cent. But still it needed to be improved and maintained continuously, for redundancy is an organic part of modern industry's growth.

The greatest step forward to achieve yard efficiency had not yet been started on. This was the Double Dayshift scheme. The yard equipment was only being used eight hours per day, five days a week, except for overtime at nights and weekdays which cost 50 per cent and 100 per cent more in labour charges. Japanese yards were using their equipment twenty-four hours a day, capitalising on investment, and making it possible for three times as many men to work on a ship with a given period of time. This meant that a ship could be constructed three times more quickly.

The Fairfields team was determined to introduce at least two shifts, with the yard building ships sixteen hours a day. The idea was to have one shift from 6 a.m. to 2 p.m. and another from 2 p.m. to 10 p.m. The service personnel, purchasing, design, work study and so on, could still remain the same, overlapping both shifts from about 8 a.m. to 5 p.m.

163

This would, again, reduce the ratio of overheads to output, improving the yard's competitiveness. This is a fairly common arrangement in many other industries in Britain, and standard in most other shipbuilding industries in the world, but was strongly resisted by the Clyde men and unions. Their resistance was based mainly on social grounds (their working day would be out of step with the routine of their families) and, of course, it would naturally mean a reduction in the amount of overtime they could earn. Fairfields was prepared to bargain over this, offering some reduction in standard hours and some increase in wage rates, for the introduction of Double Dayshift could mean such a valuable leap forward in productivity. During the night of 13–14 October 1967, negotiations with John Chalmers, Secretary of the CJC, culminated in a 4 a.m. agreement on Double Dayshift in principle but when the merger came into being Chalmers was removed from the scene.

There was therefore much to be attempted still in the Fairfields project and the thought of becoming just one of five yards in a new group, having to fit in with the ideas and methods of John Brown's, Yarrow's, Stephen's and Connell's, was anathema to every single member of the Fairfields Board. The only attractive alternative was, as stated, to absorb the other yards into Fairfields, using the Fairfields management to reorganise the others.

Furthermore, the Board genuinely believed that it was inefficient for the Clyde group to be formed through an equal merger, for they had studied the experience of Continental yards, which had shown that the only way to achieve success in mergers was for one yard to take in the others. Since then British experience seems to be proving this theory, too. Of all the rearrangements which followed Geddes, one of the more successful seems to be the Swan Hunter grouping on Tyneside which has doubled its capacity from 250 000 tons to 500 000 tons annually by purchasing the assets of Smiths Dock, John Redhead and Clelands Shipbuilding. The SIB has granted finance to help in these take-overs and the group is publishing increasing profit figures. There has been a boom in shipbuilding, due to the closure of the Suez Canal, and there is no shortage of orders, but the Upper Clyde Group has run into severe financial diffi-culties within twelve months of its formation.

Hugh Stenhouse, the Glasgow insurance tycoon, had the bit between his teeth and wanted to race around Scotland raising the cash to buy out the other yards outright especially John Brown's which might have fallen to them if enough ready money was offered to the parent company.

"One boss is essential!" he constantly hammered into the Fairfields Board table, "You can't form a merger by saying you'll please everybody. *It just won't work!"*

He was absolutely sure that Fairfields had found the solu-tion to save the Clyde, for it had succeeded in getting the labour force to work with it in comparative harmony. He appreciated that the most important asset of any company is people, and he had seen how the workers were coming more and more to follow Stewart's leadership. Management and money were necessary to make a firm prosper, but they were useless without the co-operation of the men.

The spirit of co-operation had been so strongly created at Fairfields that the whole mixed Board was confident they could continue the experiment successfully on a larger scale, with 13 000 men instead of 3000. "If it had been a question of doing a takeover, the Board would not have flinched," is Lord Carron's view still.

Iain Stewart was becoming aware that he himself was such a controversial figure, (severely resented by the other ship-builders on the Clyde,) that it would not be a practicable suggestion for Fairfields to spearhead the merger under his Chairmanship. He therefore sent the following letter to Sir William Swallow in the earliest days of the merger negotia-tions, offering to resign if Fairfields could be used as the basis for taking over the Upper Clyde. This letter was written

after the SIB members had had informal talks with the
Chairmen of the five yards, but before the Hepper Working
Party had arrived in Glasgow. Swallow had written to each
yard Chairman, saying: "The key to success is, of course,
the right choice of a chairman for the new company, and I
am sure that you have come to the right conclusion in agreeing that we should try to find a top-class industrialist with a
record of successful management of large industrial organisations and that we should look for such a man from outside
the shipbuilding companies on the Clyde. The new chairman
would of course be the chief executive and would thus be
full time. If you are in agreement with this perhaps we
could go on to discuss who might be invited to fill this
role." Stewart wrote:

23 March 1967

Dear Sir William,
In anticipation of having a discussion about the
new Chief Executive which was referred to in your
letter of 8 March, I had intended to refer to my
own particular position at yesterday's meeting. For
obvious reasons it was not appropriate to do so but
in retrospect I thought it might still be helpful to
your Board and perhaps remove some question
marks which may be in the minds of the proposed
Working Party, if I were to write to you as follows.
Firstly I should explain that my purpose in
becoming involved with the Fairfield revival was
three-fold.

1 To try and bring an end to the closure of inefficient Yards and establish that Shipbuilding
   can be competitive and profitable under efficient
   Management.
2 That in a different setting the Trade Unions
   would develop new attitudes towards flexibility
   and interchangeability and would co-operate

with Management in establishing profit through improved productivity as a common objective.

3 That in the belief that employers must have freedom to adjust their labour force according to the demand for their product that retraining and planned re-employment on a National scale must eventually be provided for redundant workers as an alternative to unemployment.

As you know we have been able to make some valuable progress on all counts but are still far from being home and dry in any of them.

In the belief that it is in the best interests of Shipbuilding that these mergers should be progressed as soon as possible, and also that the principles for which Fairfields was set up, and which have been so fully set out in the Geddes Report, should be extended, it seems to me:

1 That Fairfields may well provide you with a convenient starting point by changing the Company's name to Clyde Shipbuilders Limited.

2 That there would be very considerable advantages for the new Chief Executive and his aides to have a physical base in an existing yard on the Upper Reaches.

These existing facilities would pave the way for him, in conjunction with the Unions, to apply modern techniques and the existing Management Services Organisation over a much wider area. It would also I believe enable the Shipbuilding Industry Board to pursue more effectively and to take advantage of the not unattractive discussions which are already in progress between Fairfields and other shipbuilders. Indeed, as I pointed out at our meeting, if we had Barclay's or other berths at our disposal right now, Fairfields would be in a favourable position to obtain additional contracts which are likely to be available, e.g. for further container ships, in which we have been fortunate in being able to establish a lead position.

At our Board Meeting this morning it was clear that if we could re-arrange the berthing of our existing programme more ships could be accommodated and this, of course, would be very much to the advantage of the Clyde area as a whole.

If the above proposal would prove to be attractive to your Board I would be quite prepared to vacate the Chairmanship at Fairfields in order to make way for the early installation of your new full-time Chief Executive, and would willingly work with him to promote my original purpose, as indicated above, in a non-executive part-time capacity.

Naturally, at this stage the contents of this letter are only known to the Fairfield Board and have their unanimous approval, and particularly so in view of the need for dealing urgently with the present unsettled conditions on the Clyde.

Should, however, you wish to talk further about this I would be very glad to come and see you. All being well I expect to be in London on Tuesday, Wednesday and Thursday of next week and will be staying at the Dorchester Hotel.

Kind regards.

Yours sincerely,

Iain Stewart

PS   I think you may find that this idea would be acceptable to Barclay's and the other builders with whom we have had discussions.

These proposals by Stewart to resign and allow an outside Chief Executive to take over Fairfields and operate from there were completely rejected by Sir William Swallow. He replied:

> The other members of the Board and I are of the opinion that, because of the particular circumstances of shipbuilding in the area, the best chance of forming a group lies in approaching the problem from the outside and setting up a new company entirely separate from the existing companies. This of course is the basis of the proposals which we have been discussing with yourself and the principals of four other companies on the Upper Clyde.
>
> As regards the headquarters of a shipbuilding group, Geddes suggested that this could be either in one of the yards or separate from any of them. But we are firmly of the opinion that in a group of that proposed for the Upper Clyde, it should be separate.
>
> *William Swallow*

(In the event, the UCS Headquarters were established in a new office tower block in the centre of Glasgow, completely remote from any of the yards. The block, called Fitzpatrick House, is referred to by the men as "the Kremlin.")

This approach was obviously a blind alley for Stewart. When the Working Party arrived in April, the Fairfields Board saw that their yard would be inevitably drawn into the merger on terms they would all wish to avoid. Another last-ditch effort was made to get the plan going to buy John Brown's and so create a position of strength for Fairfields before the merger was settled. But this could not be done in time. The other three yards got wind of it and hurried their movements towards a merger on the lines being suggested by the SIB Working Party. Time ran out. The Working Party

169

Report was circulated, the management and production facilities research was completed and the Fairfields Board were
now faced with only one possibility—making the most of
the situation which now existed, achieving the best possible
settlement for Fairfields as one of the five yards. Hugh
Stenhouse still pushed the idea of going it alone, without any
of the other yards, but Derek Palmar in particular had the
task of conveying to Fairfields the wishes of the Government
and these left no doubt that the Company would have an
extremely rough time if it did not follow the recommendations of the SIB.

"Fairfields," says Palmar, "was set up in the context of
Geddes and Geddes meant a merger with the other yards.
It was quite impossible for Fairfields to have a predominant
position in the merger, because of the prejudice of the other
shipyard owners. They would never have agreed to a merger
under Fairfield leadership. It was a deplorable situation, but
there was no real and practicable alternative. It was a sacrifice, but within the context in which it was set up originally
by the Government."

When the terms were finally drawn up, some members of
the Fairfields Board were not happy about the terms offered
to Yarrow and could not see the justification for Yarrow's
retaining 49 per cent of the equity of their own company.

Behind the scenes feelings ran high, but to the public
everything was going very smoothly. Nobody wanted to risk
spoiling the image of the new group which would need as
much confidence as it could possibly muster, especially when
it came to selling the new set-up to the labour force.

So, Fairfields Board finally, on 31 October 1967, accepted
the details of the merger settlement, the £350 000 for shareholders and the 35 per cent of the equity of the UCS
group, and made the following minute:

> The Board, although not happy with certain aspects
> of the proposals, is not prepared to bear the sole

responsibility for the merger breaking down because it believes that it is in the best interests of the Company and of shipbuilding on the Clyde that the merger should proceed.

It was hardly a joyous announcement, hardly that of a bride looking eagerly forward to the wedding.

Chapter nine

Out Goes Stewart

One of the conditions that the Fairfields Board had insisted on was that Stewart should be a Deputy Chairman in the UCS grouping. The yards had agreed to Tony Hepper's taking the jobs of Chairman and Managing Director. Hepper became the outsider with experience of organisation in other industries whom Swallow agreed should be sought to fill the post of Chief Executive. None of the Chairmen of the yards was acceptable to the others for that position.

Taking the view that three Deputy Chairmen were too many, Hepper first proposed that Sir Eric Yarrow and Sir Charles Connell should be his *two* Deputy Chairmen. Stewart did not take very kindly to that and saw to it that he became one of the *three*. The other Directors on the main UCS Board were Jim Stephen of Stephen's yard, Tom Burleigh, Vice Chairman of John Brown's parent group, and M O ("Peter") Hughes, of Wallace Attwood's, the management consultants. Hughes had been one of John Rannie's negotiating team when they had met Fairfields in London to investigate possible amalgamation a few months previously.

UCS was officially formed with this Board on St Andrews Day, 30 November 1967. In February, 1968, the following additional Board appointments were announced: James Duff, to come from English Electric as Production Director;

H L Farrimond, coming from Imperial Metal, part of the ICI group, to be Personnel Director; John Starks, Assistant Managing Director of John Brown's yard to be the UCS Technical Director; R A Williamson, a Director of John Brown's yard, to be the UCS Financial Director; and John Rannie, soon to retire as Managing Director of John Brown's, to be Special Director in charge of the completion of QE2. No appointment was announced for the job of running Management Services (Productivity Services). None of Stewart's team had been given a post on the main Board, which was now very heavily weighted with men who could not be regarded as favourable to the Fairfields experiment.

Most members of the Fairfields Board now felt that they had been completely outmanoeuvred by the other four yards. No account had been taken in the executive appointments of Fairfields' management achievements or of the fact that Fairfields had been allocated the largest block of shares, 35 per cent. As the pattern became more clear, individuals tried to take action at a higher level, above the heads of the SIB and the UCS Board. Andrew Cunningham, Fairfields Director and Northern District Secretary of the General and Municipal Workers Union, sent a stinging emotional letter direct to Wedgwood Benn at the Ministry of Technology. It summed up all the frustration and bitter disappointment of the Fairfield pioneers. In it he said:

Rt Hon Anthony Wedgwood Benn
Minister of Technology   15 January 1968

You should also remember that the Fairfields experiment was based on the assumption that there would be co-operation between the government, the appointed directors and the directors appointed by the trade unions who have invested nearly £$\frac{1}{4}$ million in the concern. This experiment in my

173

opinion was not only working well but was a beacon for the rest of the shipbuilding industry in Great Britain as far as management/employee relations and efficiency was concerned, therefore it is a bad political decision to force Fairfields into this proposed merger and the terms of the merger . . .

What should have been proposed was that Fairfields as the most efficient yard should have been used as the base firm for taking over the other firms and capital should have been provided for this. No doubt your advisers will inform you that Monsieur Ravaille, the European expert on the rationalisation of shipyards on the Continent, has stated quite categorically that mergers are not practical and that the most practical approach is for the best managed shipyard to take over the yards progressively, starting with the strongest and ending with the weakest. . . .

It is quite impossible to merge old family style managements and the new style professional management which has come to be accepted in Fairfields. You will know when the clash comes the professional management who we are so anxious to retain will have to seek other jobs.

I would also like to point out that under the proposed merger, despite the fact that the unions have heavily invested themselves they are not going to be allowed a union director. This of course is probably none of your business, but it is a manifestation of the old Bourbon thinking about the whole matter.

Andrew Cunningham

In his reply to Cunningham's letter, Wedgwood Benn played his role of complete personal non-involvement—a tragic stance to be taken by a Labour Government Minister who, as head of the great new Ministry of Technology, was supposed to be lighting the way forward for rapid development of new ideas in industry and who was heir to the achievements of Fairfields created through the efforts of George Brown. Wedgwood Benn tried so hard to avoid any possible accusation of being prejudiced in favour of the Government-sponsored yard, Fairfields, that he took no account of the value of the pioneering work there and left it in the hands of some of the people it had been aiming to prove wrong.

Wedgwood Benn rejected any of the alternatives proposed by Cunningham and said:

> Because of the collapse of the old Fairfield company just before the Geddes Committee reported, the Government were glad to be able to support the Fairfield experiment in management and labour relations, but, having accepted the Geddes Report, we made it clear that we hoped Fairfields would participate in an Upper Clyde grouping on the lines proposed in the Report, and we certainly understood that this was accepted by the Board as a desirable development for the Clyde and Fairfields."

Having forced Fairfields into a situation where they were left with no alternative, the Government Minister was now accepting at face value the Fairfields Board's grudging acceptance of the inevitable!

Iain Stewart at one stage still had hopes of salvaging some sort of future for his experiment. He still retained a faith in fair play and some verbal assurances which was strangely trusting considering his wide business experience. He was playing tit for tat, but after he had given tit, he got no tat. He was totally convinced that the Fairfields achievements would be thoroughly investigated, recognised and continued under the same team on behalf of the whole UCS group. He had received promises that UCS would follow "the best proven practices on the Clyde." This had been included in a UCS statement to the Press, the relevant paragraph written by Stewart himself. Iain Stewart imagined that Fairfields was so obviously initiating the best possible practices for the Clyde that, when brought to light no one would doubt it. He saw his job on the UCS Board as one of supervising the implementation of his new management philosophy inside the bigger grouping in close collaboration with the unions and with the assistance of his former executives. He had issued a Chairman's Message in November 1967 to the Press, which was published alongside messages from the other yard Chairmen, in a special issue of *Fairfield News* which appeared as *Upper Clyde News*. This was Stewart's message:

> On 6 November the five Clyde Chairmen, their selected Board colleagues and their Financial Advisers, met in London to consider the financial proposals for integration which had been worked out as a result of several earlier discussions.
>
> On behalf of the Fairfield Board I was able to state that, although we did not think that enough weight had been given to the potential savings which would be generated from a wider application of our Management Services and our Productivity Agreements, we were prepared to recommend acceptance of the scheme to our shareholders provided that the Ministry of Technology—as one of our shareholders—and the Shipbuilding Industry Board, had no objections. This formula was eventually endorsed by all concerned and consequently the merger is an accomplished fact as soon as the Employment Charter has been signed.
>
> While in many ways it is to be regretted that it

will not be possible to complete all the experiments which have been undertaken in Fairfields, the Board of Directors is unanimously of the opinion that it is in the best interests of the Clyde as a whole that our Company should be a member of the New Group rather than continue to operate as an independent unit in isolation.

At this stage it is worth recalling that in January 1966 the three main principles which we undertook to demonstrate in our Industrial Proving Ground were as follows:

1 That with good communications the traditional craft unions would co-operate with modern Management techniques in the promotion of high productivity.
2 That in such a setting a single shipbuilding unit, such as Fairfields, could be viable in the face of international competition.
3 That redundancy, when combined with retraining and guaranteed continuity of income through planned re-employment, could become a respectable feature of industrial activity.

Facts and figures are readily available to reveal that the roots of these first two principles are well and truly planted in the Clyde area, and I am satisfied that the third can be easily achieved through a Group activity as through Fairfields itself.

It is my intention, therefore, to support the new enterprise and Mr Hepper, its Chairman, in the capacity of Non-Executive Deputy Chairman until it is evident that the Fairfield principles, its know-how and its personnel have been properly cemented into the new organisation.

In fact, the proof of the Fairfield pudding will be in the eating of it and I hope to stay on as a Deputy Chairman of the New Board until the essential ingredients have been thoroughly digested.

Iain Stewart, however, as he sat on the UCS Board surrounded by so many representatives of the other yards, outvoted constantly on every issue which he considered of vital importance realised what it really felt like to be the black sheep in the pen. There was a very, very wide divergence of opinion on what should be interpreted as "the best proven practices on the Clyde." Fighting a rearguard action now, Stewart approached Aubrey Jones, and asked if the Fairfields Experiment could be referred to the Prices and Incomes Board. Stewart hoped that an official Government inquiry into the Fairfields systems and achievements might serve to gain recognition for the value of the work done on a national scale and also ensure that the experiment was not forsaken by UCS.

Aubrey Jones was very receptive to the idea and asked the Secretary of State for Economic Affairs if this inquiry could be carried out. But that avenue was blocked by the reply from Peter Shore, who by then had been given the task of running George Brown's old Ministry.

Secretary of State for Economic Affairs
Storey's Gate London SW1
28 February 1968

Dear Aubrey,
Possible Reference of Fairfields to the NBPI
You wrote to me on 1 February suggesting that the success of the Fairfields experiment was such that a reference of it to the NBPI might be desirable before it becomes merged in the Upper Clydeside Shipbuilders Limited, in the hope that

178

this would avoid the dilution of the benefits following from the experiment. You also point out as a subsidiary advantage that this would bring the Fairfields model into greater prominence.

I have carefully considered this but I am, on balance, against such a reference at this stage. I think the reference would not necessarily achieve the objective you have in mind, since the Upper Clydeside Shipbuilders Limited have already stated publicly that they intend to adopt the best proven practices and have negotiated a cash payment to Fairfields shareholders in respect of their contribution to productivity. The Ministry of Technology and the Shipbuilding Industry Board intend to watch this point closely and there is no doubt that competent management in UCS will have to deal with the problem of the inefficient use of labour as a very high priority if there is to be any hope of the consortium becoming a viable enterprise. I am also very conscious of the difficult practical situation which has to be handled from day to day following the merger and the objections which can be urged against a reference from the point of view of adding a further task for management and the possibility that such a move might not improve relations between the various managements concerned.

You will have seen that following your letter to me there was a substantial article in the *Financial Times* of 6 February dealing with Fairfields, and my impression is that the degree of publicity attending developments there has been such that they are not likely to have been overlooked.

Yours,
Peter Shore
Right Honourable Aubrey Jones, BSc (Econ)

The late Harold Wincott of the *Financial Times* might have been amused to hear that his article was considered an adequate alternative to a Government evaluation of the Fairfields experiment! Especially as that was the article which ended with the words: "But one does fear that the verdict on the Fairfield experiment will be: 'If only we had had another two years.' It deserves a better epitaph than that." In the article, Harold Wincott had also written: "I came back from Glasgow convinced that the Fairfields experiment is succeeding and has been thoroughly worthwhile. But I have to report there is a shadow over it today—the shadow of the Upper Clyde Shipbuilders merger. Elsewhere in Scotland I heard the merger criticised on general grounds —that too much of the Shipbuilding Industry Board's money was being used to pay for assets taken *out* of the merger, and too little for modernisation and re-equipment; that in any case the money would be better spent helping, directly or indirectly, modern industries in Scotland, where her real future lies, rather than in an old and declining industry.

"I'm not pontificating on these questions. But I have to record a feeling of great disappointment and general sorrow, throughout the Fairfields business, that the Fairfields experiment can't have another two years on its own to prove its success beyond all argument. This wasn't just management talking; it was the shop stewards' unanimous view too."

What Stewart wanted, of course, with his request for a thorough Government inquiry, was not just a pat on the back and a sympathetic smile. He wanted notice to be taken by Government and Industry of the techniques of communications and negotiations and retraining which were making Fairfields a success. It was not just a question of wiping the slate clean with a payment for productivity improvements to the shareholders, a cheer from Harold Wincott and an eventual Knighthood from Harold Wilson (which he got). Fairfields was not an end in itself, but only the stepping stone to lusher pastures for the whole of British industry.

This was the feeling of his whole Fairfield team, which had not joined him just for the sake of a job in a shipyard. Jim Houston made this clear when he discussed his future position with Tony Hepper and Peter Hughes who were interviewing for the top jobs at UCS. Houston explained that he had gone to Fairfields because of the challenge of trying management techniques to revive a bankrupt shipyard. He would be interested to stay on with UCS only if he were able to continue this challenge by supervising the implementation of productivity services from the main group Board. He would not be interested in merely acting as a manager inside one division of the new group. During one of the interviews, Hepper congratulated Houston on being awarded the Gilbreth Medal for outstanding services to productivity and work study. This medal was awarded by the Institute of Work Study Practitioners and was its highest accolade.

The Working Party's report into the management and technical resources of the proposed UCS group had listed thirteen senior appointments which would have to be made. The thirteenth was a "Director of Management Services." The specification for this job had been laid down by the consultants as:

Management Services Director.
To provide assistance, advice and service throughout the Company with the application of modern management techniques. These will include planning and production control based on the use of network analyses and models, production engineering, quality control, value engineering and work measurement including methods, layout and incentives.

This was a perfect description of the work Jim Houston had been doing at Fairfields and for which he had just received the distinctions of the Gilbreth Medal.

Iain Stewart took it for granted that the job would go to Jim Houston and he was banking on being able to work with him on the UCS Board in implementing the techniques as before. Stewart, therefore, concurred at the UCS meetings as they worked through the list of the other twelve senior executive appointments, bringing in James Duff as Production Director, Farrimond as Personnel Director and giving plum Board appointments to old John Brown's men. John Starks became Technical Director, Williamson got the job of Financial Director. Then, at last, came the time to talk about the Management Services Director, or Productivity Director.

To Stewart's amazement, Jim Houston was turned down for the job by Hepper, Yarrow, Connell, Stephen, Burleigh and Hughes.

Jim Houston had made a name for himself at Fairfields which has since been recognised by some of the highest ranking organisations in industry. In addition to gaining the Gilbreth Award, he has been appointed as Chairman of the Joint Industry Board for improving labour relations and productivity in the Electrical Contractors Industry. As a consultant, he is helping to introduce a comprehensive management services department into one of Europe's largest machine tool companies. He has been appointed Productivity Adviser to the Newspaper Publishers Association, one of the key posts in the field.

The independent report by P-E Consulting Group Limited and Thomson McLintock and Company, which was produced in January 1968 and which reviewed developments in productivity in the Fairfields yard, had calculated the productivity increase at 30 per cent since the introduction of the Measured Daywork scheme and overall at 10 per cent above the highest previous figure achieved by the yard in 1964. That increase had been achieved by Houston's emergency measures within eighteen months of taking over a bankrupt and demoralised yard. Houston, one of Britain's most experienced authorities in the field of applied productivity techniques, was already in the UCS group but was not considered sufficiently capable to be given the job of handling productivity services for it, whilst, the Fairfields Board noted bitterly, John Brown's was the source of two key executive appointments and two non-executive directorships.

The Fairfields Board held its last meeting, before handing over the reins completely to UCS, in February 1968. Stewart had to report to them all that he could make no headway with his colleagues on the UCS Board and that Jim Houston was not going to be offered a senior appointment. Oliver Blanford, too, had been passed over. Blanford had asked if he could be given some overall responsibility, as Director of The South Bank Divisions, Linthouse and Govan (Stephen's and Fairfields), but the most he could be offered was the management of the Fairfields yard under Duff.

As a protest and with little hope of succeeding, the Board, with its dying gasp, made one last Board Resolution. This was:

> The Fairfields Board affirms its belief in the principles and practices of the Fairfield Experiment which has made a substantial improvement in efficiency, attitudes and relationships in the Company. It welcomes the assurance from the Chairman and Board of UCS that the Fairfield success will be carried forward and applied by the new Company. As part of this application the Board is convinced the Management Services has a key role to play and must be represented at main Board level to be fully effective. Against the background of experience at Fairfields whose shareholders will collectively have approximately 32 per cent of the shareholding in UCS, the Fairfields Board believes the control of Management Services at main Board level should be offered to Mr J D Houston. This

appointment taken together with Mr Blanford's continuing responsibility for the operation of the Govan yard will provide recognition of Fairfields' success so far and of the contribution which Fairfields' principles and practices can make to the success of Upper Clyde Shipbuilders Limited.

Iain Stewart informed his Fairfields colleagues that he would present this resolution to the next meeting of the UCS Board and that, if they did not take action on it, then he would have no alternative but to resign, for there would then be no hope of continuing the Fairfields work on a group basis. The Board accepted his recommendation that Professor Alexander should take his place in this event.

The UCS Board turned down the Fairfields request and Iain Stewart was out.

Chapter ten

Looking Back in Sorrow

Iain Stewart was perhaps the only member of the Fairfields Board who was stunned by the UCS refusal to offer Jim Houston or Oliver Blanford a top job. He was the only one of that varied bunch of experienced men who appeared to think that there would be any give and take after the UCS Board had been officially created.

Oliver Blanford had been shrewd enough to foresee the end before he had even joined Fairfields. When he was asked to take on the job of Fairfields' Chief Executive, on that plane journey from London with Iain Stewart, he had been working for several years in Glasgow industry, two of them as director in charge of engineering under Jim Stephen. "I never underestimated the power of the families," he confesses, "so even then I made sure my contract allowed me a get-out if they ever managed to take control of Fairfields. I had it written into my contract by Stewart that I would not be obliged to continue at the yard if anyone was ever brought into a position of executive authority over me. I thought that Stewart had every chance of succeeding with his managerial experiment in the yard, but only a one in four chance of beating the local vested interests. I knew they would get back."

Oliver Blanford did not stay on with UCS. He took compensation under the terms of his contract and then went to a chicken farm in the far north of Scotland to brood.

"Jim Houston is a go-getter. He has worked his way up from nowhere," Blanford remarks, "he saw the whole system on the Clyde was backward and inefficient and, to crown it all, he was right. The other yards could forgive him anything except that. You can't be worse than right."

Of Stewart, Oliver Blanford says: "Iain was too blue-eyed. He had no clue of the bitterness he had stirred up trying to pour new wine into the old bottles." During the scrummages, Oliver Blanford tried several times, but without success, to gain an audience with Wedgwood Benn.

Lord Carron, Bank of England Director and former chief of the AEU, remembers that he was "not completely surprised by the UCS refusal to give a position of authority to Jim Houston, but very chagrined. It meant the loss of the formidable productivity team we had built up and it meant that the productivity aspects of UCS would be less assured. Jim was a dynamic person for getting things doing on work evaluation and measurement. What we had done at Fairfields looked so promising. If only we could have taken over the others and carried on that work. The possibilities that had to be sacrificed were substantial, but we wanted a successful Clyde shipbuilding industry and we hoped it would be for the best. It was disappointing to say the least, that we had to give Fairfields up to a merger. It would have been far more satisfying to have gone on and proved it. It was a pity to have to give some kind of evaluation of the project before it was complete. Fairfields was a meaningful pattern for the future—for all three interests, Government, Unions and Private Investors, exist so powerfully in our mixed economy, in our type of society. Terrific prejudices existed and brought bias to bear against Fairfields from other interests, from other shipbuilders.

"Iain Stewart's philosophy was just not acceptable to some

people, but his idealism is practical idealism, not just text-book stuff, but based on practical foundations. The vested interests were concerned about the effects of his ideas on their own ivory castles. He caused fear in many circles.

"We entered into negotiations about the merger with the greatest possible reluctance, but we were obliged to merge and we then had to try to get the best possible terms to try to safeguard the Fairfield achievements."

Hugh Stenhouse was sure that Iain Stewart had "no hope in hell" of achieving anything once he went on to that UCS Board with the others. "The entire Fairfields Board believed, without exception, in the principles of Fairfields and in Iain's leadership. Iain can get away with murder with the rank and file. The yard men were in the palm of his hand. He was a persuasive, progressive leader. It was a wrong moment for the experiment to come to an end. We should have had a longer time. We argued like mad against the merger. We would have preferred to take over the others instead. Once the merger was inevitable we put our shoulder to that wheel and pushed like hell to do the best we could for that. But it was a terribly difficult time, for there were generations of rivalry involved and we were all supposed to act in unison. UCS will do an excellent job in time, but it was a pity it had to be put into the hands of the Club. It is vital for the Clyde men to trust their management. Since the 'thirties the men have been reluctant to show this trust. Fairfields had the men coming with it. Obviously this movement must have been checked."

The Jim Houston affair was not the sole reason, of course, for Iain Stewart's resignation from the Board of UCS. It was for him the last straw. His views on what UCS should do as a priority differed fundamentally from what the rest of the UCS Board were proposing to do. Although Stewart had been able to win the confidence of the Fairfield workers right from the start, he had never tried to achieve this through any soft or over-conciliatory measures. His policy had been to "hold them over a barrel," make them see how much in the mire they were, show them how to get out of it and then offer them the guarantee of better conditions and greater security in return for guarantees from their side, too. There was always a bargain, nothing for nothing. He had not offered guaranteed employment until the labour force had been cut down to the numbers he reckoned to be right for the work, reducing the number of jobs by about 750 in the first seven or eight months. He had then guaranteed an income to the remainder, secure in the knowledge that he had the end of demarcation under his belt and a reasonably sound guarantee of no strikes. He had also set up the training facilities to make it possible to retrain men from a redundant section to play a useful role in another section of the yard. In the end, there would be no fear of unemployment.

Throughout all the preliminaries of the Fairfields experiment, Stewart had avoided filling the order book too full, so that the threat of unemployment loomed during the "educational" period as a real possibility. His maxim had been "Cut the work force to the right size and shape, train it to full peak and then load it with just the right type of work."

The UCS policy, however, was to fly off as rapidly as possible and bring back the orders. In a very short time Hepper was able to bring back orders worth over £60 million, some suggested by other UK shipbuilders to be at no more than cost price. With the group orders on hand, that brought the total up to around £90 million, not counting the £30 million worth of QE2 which was in the final stages of construction.

Stewart constantly cried out, "Get the labour signed up and tell them your plans first!" but the reply always was that without orders there was no future and no UCS. There was to be no Union representative on the Board. Stewart's concern was that once the order coffers were full, the men in their current mood and with fears of yard closures would have the upper hand over the employers and there would be no strength to the UCS Board's bargaining arm. The men would hold the management over the barrel. There could then be no certainty that any orders would work out at a profit.

UCS also in the very earliest days, to escape from an immediate threat of labour unrest and uncertainty, gave a guarantee of two years employment to almost the total labour force of about 12 000 men from the five yards, yet the consultants' definite recommendation had been that the group could only become efficient and viable with a payroll reduced to 7500. This in turn meant that orders, almost at any price, had to be gained in a hurry to keep so many workers busy.

Because senior UCS management became so involved with the chase after business throughout the world, less attention was given to communication with the shop stewards, the foremen and the workers. There was a dangerous hiatus between the handing over of the yards to UCS and any clear-cut indication of what was expected of each individual. The saying went round the river, "It is easier to get an audience with the Pope than to meet Tony Hepper." Hepper's answer to this was, "Let's get the orders, then we can meet and talk." But this lost the most vitally receptive period of all, the period when men have been given a new regime with all the attendant uncertainty, when they are looking for reassurance, for a leader. If the leader-to-be does not come forward at that point in time, then the gap is likely to be filled with apathy or with troublemakers. Stewart had learnt how valuable it was to grab the confidence and the co-operation of the men when they were still wondering what the new management was going to be like at Fairfields. He had addressed them all at the Lyceum before he had even formed the new company. He also had learnt how "bolshy" the men and the shop stewards had become during that unavoidable delay between announcement of the plan on 9 December 1965 and the raising of the cash on 22 December 1965.

These were lessons he felt he had learnt once and he was not able to sit on the UCS Board and watch what he considered to be mistakes being made at such a vital stage in the life of the whole Clyde industry.

The Fairfields Board had also been careful to avoid any close ties with outside organisations which would hamper its freedom of negotiation with the men and the unions. The Company had not joined the Shipbuilding Employers Federation so that it was not bound by any agreements on wages or working conditions made by that body. One of the UCS first steps was to become a member of the Federation, as all the other member yards had been, Stephen's, Connell's, Yarrow's and John Brown's. Those yards had in fact previously been between themselves the Clyde Shipbuilders Association, another body which Fairfields had avoided. UCS also fragmented the Central Joint Council by dealing separately with the Boilermakers.

Without the aid of Blanford or Houston on the main Board, outnumbered by his former critics, Iain Stewart saw no point in remaining on the Board and associating himself with policies he opposed and which he was powerless to influence. One day, just before he quit, he happened to be on the same plane as John Rankin, the Govan MP, on a flight down to London. Stewart recited the list of his troubles to him. Rankin spent an hour pleading with Stewart not to resign. "It's no good, John," said Stewart, "it's got to come. Everything I suggest is voted down. Everything we stood for is either ignored or reversed and communications have gone to hell."

From the airport, John Rankin went to see Wedgwood Benn. "I begged the Minister to make Stewart Chairman of UCS," Rankin recalls, "to keep him on, because he was the only man who could get a new spirit into shipbuilding on Clydeside. But it was no use. 'It's all been decided' was all

Benn would say to me. 'Hepper is a fine man, but who is he to the men up there?' I asked. I told him that to the men in the yards it all just looked like the re-enthronement of *the old gang*. That is what the men were calling the UCS Board. Wedgwood Benn was too new to the story. So I went to see George Brown. He shook his head. 'I'm no longer in power, John,' he told me. It was the first moment I realised how big the break was between George and his friends in the Cabinet. It is an immense pity that George was not still there at that point."

The non-Fairfields shipbuilders, of course, take a totally different view of the whole affair. They have no feeling of having been robbed. Rather they sigh with some relief at having been rescued, from financial distress and from Iain Stewart. Those still involved with the merger have their hands and heads too full of the present problems to concern themselves too much with the problems overcome in the past. Tony Hepper steadfastly plays down any offer of a "debate" on the Fairfields question, maintaining that everything was done for the best in a difficult situation and that the choicest slices of the Fairfields joint have been incorporated into the UCS diet, the gristle and rind being rejected as they come across it.

Some of the seedlings planted by Fairfields are making root and pushing up healthy growth here and there in the new environment. Group buying, for example, is being organised by former Fairfields men who found purchasing methods at the other yards "equally appalling" to those first discovered at Govan. Several of the Fairfields buying personnel have been upgraded to group status and are now engaged in introducing efficient paperwork procedures into all five divisions. They have initiated the Field Liaison Engineers system for chasing in supplies, even setting up permanent residents in the main buying areas of Birmingham and London.

John Rannie, now retired after fifty years in the industry,

freely confesses that there was much room for improvement in Clyde shipbuilding methods, but maintains that as only about 25 per cent of the cost of a ship comes from yard labour and materials, the rest being invested in outside supplies, then there is basically little to be done in reducing building costs until costs are stabilised overall throughout British industry. He agrees that labour is the most important ingredient in ship construction, but feels, very guardedly because he does not want a wrangle, that the Fairfields people were probably "a wee bit intolerant in handling the big brush. Men-management relations have to be tackled more gradually." He will not give a judgement on the Fairfields experiment, saying it did not last long enough to prove anything either way.

Jim Lenaghan, formerly the Govan yard's General Manager and for many years a shipbuilder in Belfast, regrets that Fairfields was not taken up as an experimental company to be studied by the whole shipbuilding industry. "It could have served as a research centre in new techniques, labour relations and productivity," he states. "If only certain persons had been able to see eye to eye, there might have been more lasting benefit for everyone."

Perhaps Jim Stephen, one of the shipbuilding families and a non-executive Director on the UCS Board, sums up the attitude of many like himself on the Clyde when he says: "Publicly we made no comment on Fairfields. What we said in private had better remain private."

UCS executives must naturally find it difficult to pontificate on the rights and wrongs of the Fairfields affair because they have still a long way to go before proving themselves efficient. The delay in delivering the QE2 meant that a large part of group facilities was tied up with that ship far beyond schedule, upsetting the flow of work on other ships. Several ships now under construction in the UCS yards are running well behind time. There is also a mighty problem of keeping far more than the required number of men employed. The Fairfields yard, now called the Govan Division, is packed with over 5000 men compared with about 3000 before the merger. They are still working single shift and there has been no significant increase in available equipment. Productivity must have slipped. It was therefore no surprise when the SIB refused to hand over the capital requested by the UCS Board until there had been a complete review of the prospects for improving productivity in the group.

One important customer for the Clyde yards is Reardon Smith, the Cardiff shipping company which operates a fleet of tramp cargo ships and has placed a score of orders in its time with yards around Glasgow. When Fairfield Shipbuilding went bankrupt there were two orders on hand for 25 000-ton bulk carriers. George Brown personally called Bob Chatterton, the Reardon Smith Chief Executive, to ask him to renew the orders with the new Company he was trying to form. Chatterton agreed. New contracts were signed and new delivery dates given. For the first time for many years, Reardon Smith had its ships delivered without any delay in the promised schedule. As described earlier, *Atlantic City* was handed over on time to the very day, whilst the second ship, *Indian City,* was one week early. Consequently, further orders were placed with the same yard. *Welsh City* was then handed over to the Cardiff owners on time, just a few days after the yard had become part of the UCS grouping. However, one year later, the situation had changed very much for the worse. *Cornish City,* launched in April 1969, is now due for delivery over two months later than originally promised, whilst another bulk carrier, as yet unnamed, is already running four months behind schedule.

For the first time, Reardon Smith are considering going to foreign yards to place their next orders, because they simply cannot afford the financial losses resulting from late delivery of ships. Although there are penalty clauses in the contracts, they have never yet taken them up because of the legal complications and covers. Besides, they say, the compensation payments would in no way meet the losses flowing from interest payments on cash laid down for ships which are not yet in operation. An overdue ship is an idle ship, costing money and earning nothing. There has never been any criticism from Reardon Smith of the quality of Clyde-built ships. They consider them to be the finest in the world, but only the new Fairfields operated management control in the way that they would like to see introduced everywhere. "We learnt a lot, too," confesses Bob Chatterton. "Ship-owners were just as guilty as shipbuilders in being behind the times. Our late Chairman, for example, could say, 'It's time we had a new ship. The last one did pretty well. Let's have another like that.' But those days have gone. Now-adays we have to send a team round the world to research the future requirements for cargo ships, so that we have ships built to gain maximum profit into the future. I used to like going up to Fairfields to talk to Stewart and Blanford and Houston about new methods of management control and we are implementing many of their suggestions here in Cardiff."

The ripples from Fairfields are spreading through UK industry, even if not in the massive waves which Stewart had planned. Derek Palmar, immediately Fairfields merged, became Chairman of the SIB Working Party which went to organise a grouping of three shipbuilding companies on the River Wear. Careful to avoid the errors of the Clyde merger, he did not try to force through a formula which was not completely suited to and acceptable to all three parties. The final result was that the biggest company there, Doxford's, remained independent, going it alone on a sudden influx of new orders resulting from Government credit terms for UK-built ships for UK owners. The other two yards merged, the larger one, Austin and Pickersgill, being the dominant partner over the much smaller yard of Bartram's. Many of Fairfields lessons have been passed on through Palmar to the new group management.

Jim Houston left shipbuilding after being on the receiving end of some hard knocks. On one occasion he was accused of trying to foment a strike at the Govan yard! It seems there might have been a misunderstanding arising from Houston's earlier efforts to introduce Double Dayshift working which was still resisted by most of the men. On an earlier occasion, whilst Stewart was still a member of the UCS Board, the directors had summoned Houston to their presence to complain that he was guilty of a "breach of proper conduct." His misdemeanour?—joining the shop stewards for tea instead of joining the management during a break in negotiations. Apparently some members of the group Board were against this kind of "fraternisation" with the "other side."

On the occasion of this upbraiding in the Board Room at the Connell yard (being used temporarily by UCS), Houston complained that he had been made to wait for one hour alone in a bare room with just the wall to look at. "It was like being in a concentration camp," said Houston.

Jim Houston left UCS and set up his own consultancy, Higher Productivity (Organisation and Bargaining) Limited, in partnership with four of the productivity managers from his Fairfields team. They invited Iain Stewart to be Chairman and he accepted and invested some money in it personally. The HPL team is now lecturing throughout Britain and introducing their crash-programme methods into a variety of industries with astonishingly rapid success. They have tackled transport, foundries, machine tools and newspaper publishing, but not shipbuilding, since.

When Iain Stewart was offered his Knighthood "as ex-Chairman of Fairfields (Glasgow) Limited" he thought for a long time, many days, before accepting it from a Labour Government which had betrayed his and their own experiment, but he finally accepted it so that it would be another fact of recognition that Fairfields had existed as a national proving ground. In their short blaze of limelight, he and his men feel they sent out a sufficient number of sparks to burn up some of the deadwood which covers so much of British industrial management. In an article in *The Times* in April 1968, Stewart wrote: "I have always believed that it is better to light a candle rather than curse the darkness." On the whole he blamed the Government for allowing the Fairfields flame to be snuffed out prematurely, but he has also blamed it on "a mixture of incompetence, ignorance, arrogance, laziness and prejudice."

George Brown refuses to give his views on the end of the project which cost him so much effort to start.

"I am not going to comment," he says, "on the stupid things this Government has done since I left it."

Fairfields Who's Who

*A brief background to some of the people who
played an important role in the Fairfields story*

FAIRFIELDS. The shipyard is situated in the Govan district
of Glasgow, on the south bank of the upper reaches of the
Clyde. Origins can be traced back as far as 1834, but the
first ship was built in 1860. In 1886 it was registered as The
Fairfield Shipbuilding and Engineering Company, having
built the liner *Arizona* in 1879 which held the Blue Riband
of the Atlantic.

The shipyard constructed a considerable number of
famous naval and merchant ships under a number of different
owners, and was particularly prosperous immediately prior
to and during the Second World War under control of members of the Lithgow family. It ran into financial difficulties
after the start of 1960 and the Bank of Scotland appointed a
receiver, Alex Mackenzie, in October 1965.

The Lithgows controlled a yard on the lower reaches of
the Clyde which has now become part of the Scott–Lithgow
shipbuilding consortium. The assets and existing contracts of
Fairfield Shipbuilding and Engineering Company Limited
were purchased in January 1966 by the new company,
Fairfields (Glasgow) Limited. In February 1968, the yard
was merged into the Upper Clyde Shipbuilders group, with

the four other remaining yards on the upper Clyde, John Brown's, Yarrow's, Connell's and Stephen's.

BOARD OF DIRECTORS OF FAIRFIELDS (GLASGOW) LIMITED

STEWART, *Sir* Iain Maxwell, MINA, MINE, MIMech.E. Age 53; Chairman of Fairfields (Glasgow) Limited and, briefly, Deputy Chairman of Upper Clyde Shipbuilders Limited; at present director of numerous companies, including Babcock and Wilcox, British European Airways, Dorchester Hotel, Eagle Star Insurance Company Limited, Hall-Thermotank (Chairman), Lyle Shipping, National Commercial Bank of Scotland, Scottish Television (Vice-Chairman). Former President of Institution of Engineers and Shipbuilders in Scotland, 1961–3; signatory to the Marlow Declaration.

BLANFORD, E Oliver T. Age 55; Director and General Manager of Fairfields; formerly Director of Engineering at Alexander Stephen and Sons Limited; Vice-Chairman of Confederation of British Industry's Scottish Council and Chairman of Management Research Group.

ALEXANDER, *Professor* Kenneth J W. Age 47: Professor of Economics and Head of Department of Economics, University of Strathclyde, Glasgow; Economic Consultant to Clyde Port of Authority; was a member of the Advisory Committee on the University of the Air; now a director of Upper Clyde Shipbuilders Limited.

CARRON, *Baron* William John. Director of Bank of England; 1956–67 President of Amalgamated Engineering Union; former Chairman of British Productivity Council; Member of Executive Council of Shipbuilding and Engineering Unions; member Joint Council of TUC. Signatory to the Marlow Declaration.

CUNNINGHAM, Andrew, JP. Northern District Secretary of General and Municipal Workers Union.

HOUSTON, James D. Age 46; Director of Productivity Services at Fairfields; formerly Director of Engineering, Singer Sewing Machines, Clydebank; now Managing Director of Higher Productivity (Organisation and Bargaining) Limited; Vice-Chairman, Glasgow Productivity Association; awarded 1968 Gilbreth Medal by Institute of Work Study Practitioners; Chairman of Joint Industry Board for the Electrical Contractors Industry; Productivity Adviser to Newspaper Publishers Association.

LENAGHAN, James. Former Director and General Manager of Fairfield Shipbuilding and Engineering; Past President of Institution of Engineers and Shipbuilders in Scotland, 1966–8.

PALMAR, Derek James. Age 50; Director of Hill Samuel and Company Limited, Merchant bankers; formerly Industrial Adviser to Department of Economic Affairs; Chairman of Shipston Automation Limited and Director of several other companies.

SCAMP, *Sir* Jack. Personnel Director, GEC; Chairman of Motor Industry Joint Labour Council; Member of 1964 Lord Devlin Committee of Inquiry into Docks; 1965–6 Industrial Adviser to Department of Economic Affairs; Chairman of 1969 Inquiry into Barrow shipyard demarcation dispute.

STENHOUSE, Hugh. Age 54; Chairman of Stenhouse Holdings Limited; Chairman, Great Northern Investment Trust Limited; Chairman, John Wallace and Sons Limited; Director of numerous other companies. Former Member of East Kilbride Development Board.

POLITICIANS AND PUBLIC SERVANTS

BROWN, *Rt Hon*, George Alfred, PC, MP for Belper. Deputy Leader of Labour Party; October 1964 to August 1966 First Secretary of State and Secretary of State for Economic Affairs; 1966–68 Secretary of State for Foreign Affairs; Director of Courtaulds Limited.

BUCHANAN, Richard, MP (Labour) for Springburn Division of Glasgow.

CALLAGHAN, *Rt Hon*, James, MP, PC. Secretary of State for Home Affairs; formerly Chancellor of the Exchequer.

BENN, *Rt Hon* Anthony Wedgwood, MP, PC. Minister of Technology since 1966.

HANNAN, William, MP (Labour) for Maryhill Division of Glasgow. PPS to George Brown at DEA and Foreign Office.

JONES, *Rt Hon* Aubrey, PC. Chairman of National Prices and Incomes Board; Former Minister of Fuel and Power; Minister of Supply; Chairman of Staveley Industries Limited; Director of GKN Steel Company; Director of Courtaulds Limited.

MILLAN, Bruce, MP (Labour) for Craigton Division of Glasgow.

SWALLOW, *Sir* William. Chairman of Shipbuilding Industry Board; former Chairman of Vauxhall Motors and President of Society of Motor Manufacturers and Traders.

RANKIN, John, MP (Labour Co-op) for Govan Division of Glasgow. Teacher and graduate of Glasgow University.

LEVER, Harold, MP (Labour). Financial Secretary to the Treasury.

MAXWELL, Robert, MC, MP, (Labour). Chairman of Pergamon Press and other companies.

TAYLOR, Edward Macmillan, MP (Conservative) for Cathcart Division of Glasgow. Journalist, formerly on staff of *Glasgow Herald* and Industrial Relations Officer of Clyde Shipbuilders Association, 1959–64.

OTHER INVESTORS, BUSINESS AND PUBLIC FIGURES

COLTART, James Milne. Deputy Chairman and Managing Director of The Thomson Organisation Limited; Thomson Television (International) Limited; The Scotsman Publications Limited; Chairman of Scottish Television Limited; Director of Times Newspapers Limited.

CONNERY, Sean. Star of James Bond films and many others; producer of *The Bowler and the Bunnet*; former holder of eight union cards.

CHATTERTON, Charles Robert. General Manager and Director of Reardon Smith Line Limited; Director of Anglo-American Line Limited; Leeds Shipping Company Limited; Shipping Supply Limited.

FRASER, *the late Baron* Hugh of Allander. Chairman of House of Fraser Limited; Harrods Limited; John Barker and Company Limited; George Outram and Company Limited, publishers of *The Glasgow Herald*.

JENKINS, *Dr* Carson. Lecturer and researcher at University of Strathclyde; co-author with Professor Alexander of forthcoming book on Fairfields experiment; now at University of the West Indies.

SALVESEN, *Captain* Harold. Chairman of Salvesen and Company Limited shipping lines and other companies.

THOMSON, *Baron* Roy Herbert of Fleet. Chairman of The Thomson Organisation Limited; The Scotsman Publications Limited; Thomson Newspapers Limited, Toronto, Canada; formerly Chairman of Scottish Television Limited; Director of Royal Bank of Canada.

WOLFSON, *Sir* Isaac. Chairman of The Great Universal Stores Limited. Started his business life in Glasgow.

OTHER TRADE UNIONISTS

AIRLIE, John. Fairfields Convenor of Engineering Shop Stewards.

CHALMERS, John. Secretary of the Boilermakers Society and Secretary of the Fairfields Central Joint Council.

COOPER, *Baron* J. General Secretary and Treasurer of National Union of General and Municipal Workers; Chairman of British Productivity Council 1965–6; Member of TUC General Council; signatory to Marlow Declaration.

DUFFY, William. Former Fairfields Boilermakers Shop Steward promoted to Foreman.

GALLAGHER, Harry (deceased). The late Chairman of the Clyde District Committee of the Confederation of Shipbuilding and Engineering Unions.

GRAY, George, Fairfields Convener of Boilermakers Shop Stewards.

JACK, James. General Secretary of the Scottish Trades Union Congress.

JAMIESON, Alex. Formerly Convener of Shop Stewards at Fairfield-Rowan Engineering Works and of Joint Shop Stewards Committee of Fairfield-Rowan and Fairfield yard.

KELLY, "Pat." Former Local Delegate on Clydeside of the Boilermakers' Society.

McGARVEY, Danny. President of Boilermakers Society; member of General Council TUC; member of Shipbuilding Industry Training Board and of Shipbuilding and Ship-repairing Council.

McGUINNESS, Alex. First full-time Convener of Shop Stewards at Fairfields (Glasgow) Limited and now Transfers Manager at Upper Clyde Shipbuilders Limited.

SIM, Charles. Fairfields Boilermakers Shop Steward.

BOARD OF UPPER CLYDE SHIPBUILDERS LIMITED

HEPPER, Anthony Evelyn. Age 45; Chairman and Managing Director of Upper Clyde Shipbuilders Limited (UCS); formerly Director of Thomas Tilling Limited; Industrial Adviser to the Department of Economic Affairs; Member of Shipbuilding Industry Board.

CONNELL, Sir Charles. Age 69; Deputy Chairman of UCS; Chairman of Charles Connell and Company Limited and other companies; Director of St Andrews Shipping Company; Scottish Ore Carriers Limited; G and J Weir Limited; former President of Clyde Shipbuilders Association (1949); Shipbuilding Employers' Federation (1950–1); Shipbuilding Conference (1952–3); British Employers' Confederation (1954–6).

YARROW, Sir Eric Grant, MBE. Age 59; Deputy Chairman of UCS; Chairman of Yarrow (Shipbuilders) Limited; Yarrow and Company Limited; Vice-Chairman of Standard Life Assurance Company; Director of Clydesdale Bank Limited.

ALEXANDER, *Professor* Kenneth. Non-Executive Director, UCS. (See also Board of Fairfields (Glasgow Limited.)

BURLEIGH, T H. Non-Executive Director of UCS; Managing Director of Firth Brown Tools Limited; Deputy Chairman of John Brown and Company (Clydebank) Limited and others.

HUGHES, M O. Non-Executive Director of UCS; Director of Wallace Attwood Company, management consultants.

MACKENZIE, Alexander. Government Director of UCS; Deputy Chairman of North of Scotland Hydro-Electric Board; director of several trusts and insurance firms; was Receiver appointed by Bank of Scotland to dispose of Fairfield Shipbuilding and Engineering assets.

RANNIE, John. Now retired; was Special Director of UCS in charge of completion of QE2; previously Managing Director of John Brown and Company (Clydebank) Limited.

STEPHEN, James F. Non-Executive Director of UCS; Chairman of Alexander Stephen and Sons Limited.

CORFE, J M B. Marketing Director of UCS: formerly with Shell Petroleum Company.

DUFF, James. Production Director of UCS; formerly with English Electric Company Limited.

FARRIMOND, H L. Personnel Director, UCS; formerly with Imperial Metal Industries, an ICI company.

STARKS, John. Technical Director of UCS; formerly Assistant Managing Director of John Brown and Company (Clydebank) Limited.

WILLIAMSON, R A. Financial Director of UCS; formerly Director of John Brown and Company (Clydebank) Limited.

The Fairfields
Procedure Agreement

This Agreement is made between Fairfields (Glasgow)
Limited and the following Trade Unions:

The Amalgamated Engineering Union.
The Amalgamated Society of Boilermakers, Shipwrights,
    Blacksmiths and Structural Workers.
The Amalgamated Society of Woodworkers.
The Electrical Trades Union.
The National Union of General and Municipal Workers.
The National Union of Sheet Metal Workers and Copper-
    smiths.
The Plumbing Trades Union.
The Amalgamated Society of Painters and Decorators.
The Transport and General Workers' Union.
The United Patternmakers' Association.
Draughtsmen's and Allied Technicians' Association.
Association of Supervisory Staffs, Executives and Technicians.
Clerical and Administrative Workers' Union.

—being the Unions with members currently employed by the
Company.

This Agreement rescinds all previous agreements official
and unofficial and represents a new start.

1 DEFINITIONS

(*a*) Fairfields (Glasgow) Limited, shall be referred to as "the Company."

(*b*) The above Unions and other Trade Unions who later become associated with this Agreement shall be referred to as the "Trade Unions."

(*c*) Employees shall be referred to as the "Employees," which term shall include all staff up to the rank of Head Foreman/Departmental Head.

(*d*) "Shop Steward"/Trade Union Representative shall mean the local Trade Union representative elected from employees of the Company.

(*e*) "Foreman"/Departmental Head shall mean the first line manager in shop, ship or office to whom the employee reports directly.

(*f*) "Manager" shall mean the second line manager to whom the "Foreman"/Departmental Head reports. In many cases this will be a Head Foreman or Superintendent.

2 GENERAL PRINCIPLES

(*a*) The Company requires and will encourage its employees to be members of the appropriate Trade Union.

(*b*) The Company undertake to try, on request, to provide the facility of collecting Union dues by deduction from wages and to forward a cheque to the appropriate person in each Union covering the dues collected.

(*c*) The Trade Unions recognise the right and duty of the Company to select, appoint and promote employees, Foremen/Departmental Head and Managers at the Company's discretion and make the decisions required to run the business as a commercially viable unit.

(*d*) The Company will not recruit an employee who is not a member of his appropriate Trade Union and will refer the new employee to the appropriate Shop Steward/Trade

Union representative of the department concerned as soon after recruitment as is mutually convenient.

(*e*) The Company recognises the right and obligation of the Trade Unions to exercise their functions within the framework of this agreement.

(*f*) Both parties recognise the value of consultation in their successful operation of the business and intend to act and train their officials to act, in this spirit.

3 CENTRAL JOINT COUNCIL

(*a*) There shall be a Central Joint Council consisting of Trade Union members with Executive Authority. Up to three members shall be from the Amalgamated Society of Boiler-makers, Shipwrights, Blacksmiths and Structural Workers with one member from each of the other signatory Trade Unions mentioned above and not less than three members of the management appointed by the Company. The Chairman of the Council shall be appointed by the Company.

(*b*) Meetings of the Central Joint Council shall take place at the request of either side and not less frequently than once every three months from the date of commencement of this Agreement.

Normally notice of meetings will be given between the Secretary of the Trade Union side and the Personnel Services Manager of the Company two weeks in advance and an Agenda agreed between the two of them will be circulated at the time of calling the meeting.

(*c*) The Central Joint Council may discuss any matter affecting employees of the Company and matters affecting the employers interest and shall negotiate all agreements in connection with basic wage applications and common con-ditions of employment.

(*d*) The Central Joint Council shall set up a standing sub-committee to deal with matters referred to it under Article 7(*c*). This sub-committee (with powers to co-opt) shall consist of four Trade Union members and three members appointed by Management, one of whom shall act as Chairman. The sub-committee shall appoint a secretary who will record Minutes of decisions. Normally such Minutes shall be agreed and recorded at the meeting. Failing this, the Minutes shall be circulated to members and agreed either by post or at the subsequent meeting.

4 SHOP STEWARDS/TRADE UNION REPRESENTATIVES

(a) Employees may elect an adequate number of representatives appointed from members of each of the Trade Unions employed in the establishment. These representatives shall act on behalf of the employees in accordance with the terms of this Agreement.

(b) The representatives shall be known as Shop Stewards/ Trade Union representatives.

(c) The appointment of Shop Stewards/Trade Union representatives shall be determined by each Trade Union according to its rules.

(d) The names of the Shop Stewards/Trade Union representatives appointed shall be notified in duplicate by the Trade Union concerned to the Company within a few days of the election.

The Trade Union will advise the Company in duplicate when a Shop Steward/Trade Union representative resigns or is relieved from office.

The Company will sign and return the second copy as an acknowledgement in each case.

(e) No one shall recognise any Shop Steward/Trade Union representative who has not been appointed as set out above.

(f) The Company will provide Shop Stewards/Trade Union representatives with a central meeting room in which they can meet either with employees or with Union officials on matters which arise and fall within the framework of this Agreement.

(*g*) The Shop Stewards/Trade Union representatives shall be able to leave his department to deal with relevant matters or at the request of the District Official of his Union or the Convener but he shall inform his Foreman/Departmental Head before leaving and return to work as quickly as is reasonable.

(*h*) Each Shop Steward/Trade Union representative shall be subject to the control of his Trade Union and shall act in accordance with the rules of his Union and Works rules, and in accordance with this Agreement, and with any future agreements made with the Central Joint Council or at local level with the Company.

(*i*) Management and Shop Stewards/Trade Union representatives bind themselves to do their best to avoid breaches of this Agreement and of future agreements made by the Central Joint Council or at local level.

(*j*) Action taken by Shop Stewards/Trade Union representatives in good faith while pursuing their duties as defined under this Agreement shall not in any way adversely affect their employment with the Company, and no Shop Steward/ Trade Union representative shall be dismissed for Trade Union activity.

(*k*) Shop Stewards/Trade Union representatives shall conform to the same working conditions and be subject to the same rules as their fellow employees.

(*l*) The Shop Stewards/Trade Union representatives shall elect a Convener of Shop Stewards/Trade Union representatives and two scrutineers.

5 INFORMATION

The Company undertakes to keep the men well informed about the Company, its prospects, trading conditions and policies. Management will be responsible for communicating such information together with information about the intentions and proposals of management to Shop Stewards/Trade Union representatives and to the men under their control. The Company undertakes that any negotiations resulting from this information will follow procedure laid down for the appropriate negotiation.

6 JOINT CONSULTATION

The Management and employees shall set up a sufficient number of advisory committees which are the subject of a separate agreement.

7 PROCEDURE

There shall be three procedures referring respectively to:
(*a*) Grievances affecting one or a group of employees.
(*b*) Negotiations affecting one Union.
(*c*) Negotiations affecting two or more Unions.

After completion of each stage in these procedures the senior Company official present shall draw up a report on the agreement or on the nature of the disagreement and shall forward this report to the Personnel Services Manager, the Shop Steward/Trade Union representative, the Convener of Shop Stewards/Trade Union representatives and the next senior manager in line. In addition he shall arrange, if requested, for the next step in procedure to be taken as quickly as possible.

In the event of agreement the Shop Steward/Trade Union representative and Convener will sign the report; in the event of disagreement the report shall be mutually agreed if possible; if not the Shop Steward/Trade Union representative shall submit a separate report.

7a GRIEVANCES AFFECTING ONE OR A GROUP OF EMPLOYEES

(*a*) i An employee who wishes to raise any matter in which he is directly and personally concerned shall first discuss it with his Foreman/Departmental Head in company, if the employee so desires, of his Shop Steward/Trade Union representative. In the event that a group is concerned the Shop Steward/Trade Union representative shall approach the Foreman/Departmental Head.

(*a*) ii Should the matter remain unresolved, the Foreman/ Departmental Head shall issue a report to the Personnel Services Manager who, if unable to resolve the matter himself, shall seek a meeting with the appropriate manager, the Shop Steward/Trade Union representative, the Foreman/ Departmental Head, and the men concerned, at which the Manager shall be the Chairman. This meeting shall take place as quickly as it can conveniently be arranged.

(*a*) iii Should the matter remain unresolved, the Personnel Services Manager shall report it to an executive manager, who shall be the Chairman and who will arrange for a discussion between himself, the Personnel Services Manager, the appropriate manager, Foreman/Departmental Head, Shop Steward/Trade Union representative and the man concerned.

(*a*) iv Should the matter remain unresolved then the Personnel Services Manager shall refer the matter to the Managing Director whose decision will normally be final subject to the Union(s) raising the matter through the negotiating machinery.

7b NEGOTIATION AFFECTING ONE UNION

(*b*) i This negotiation may either be started by the senior Shop Steward/Trade Union representative of the Union concerned approaching the Personnel Services Manager or by

THE FAIRFIELDS PROCEDURE AGREEMENT

the Personnel Services Manager approaching the senior Shop Steward/Trade Union representative.

(*b*) ii The Personnel Services Manager will convene a meeting as quickly as is conveniently possible between the Shop Steward/Trade Union representative concerned and the representative of the management.

(*b*) iii Should agreement not be reached, then the Personnel Services Manager will arrange a meeting between the District official of the Union and one or more senior managers. This meeting shall be called a *Local Official Conference* and shall be convened as quickly as the relevant people can be got together and the necessary information collected—normally in less than ten working days.

(*b*) iv Should agreement not be reached either the Company or the Executive Committee of the appropriate Trade Union may refer the matter to a *Scottish Conference* consisting of two or more officials of the Unions, nominated by the Central Joint Council and two members of management.

This meeting will also be convened as quickly as the relevant people and information can be got together.

(*b*) v Normally the Scottish Conference will be final but in matters of grave importance the Union concerned may be asked to call a conference which will be attended by the Managing Director or his deputy, one or two members of management and the appropriate Trade Union officials, and by invitation one or more members of the Conciliation Branch of the Ministry of Labour such conferences will be held within ten working days of Scottish Conference. Procedure at this point would be exhausted but no stoppage, overtime ban, or other limitation on production of work shall take place until this point has been reached.

7c NEGOTIATION AFFECTING MORE THAN ONE UNION

(*c*) i When a matter arises affecting more than one Union either the Convener of Shop Stewards/Trade Union representatives will approach the Personnel Services Manager or the Personnel Services Manager will approach the Convener of Shop Stewards/Trade Union representatives and a meeting shall be arranged between representatives of the Management and the representatives of the Shop Stewards/Trade Union Representatives Committee of the Unions concerned.

(c) ii Should agreement not be reached either party may refer the matter to the sub-committee of the Central Joint Council.

(c) iii Should agreement not be reached either party may invoke procedure under Clause (b) iii.

(c) iv When management wish to start negotiations about an important matter affecting more than one Union they will inform the Central Joint Council and may have informal discussions at this level.

Thereafter, they may, with the agreement of both sides, call meetings of the employees concerned to whom the relevant manager and Foreman/Departmental Head will explain what is proposed.

(c) v When the men have had time to consider the matter, the procedure set out from 7 (c) i will be followed.

(c) vi The parties agree that there shall be no stoppage of work, overtime ban or other limitation on production until procedure has been exhausted.

8 SETTLEMENTS AND AGREEMENTS

(a) The settlement arrived at during such negotiations shall be back-dated to take effect for the first complete pay week after the date of the meeting laid down in 7 (b) ii or 7 (c) i as may be appropriate.

(b) During negotiations both Management and Trade Union officials pledge themselves to try to resolve the matter as quickly and harmoniously as the circumstances of the case permit.

(c) The Unions and Company bind themselves not to enter

into agreements at shop floor level which are inconsistent with agreements made between the Central Joint Council and the Company.

9   CONTRACT OF EMPLOYMENT

This Agreement shall become part of the contract of employment of each employee from the date of signing the Agreement and each new employee shall read and sign a copy of this Agreement which thereafter shall form part of his contract of employment.

Shop Stewards/Trade Union representatives will be issued with a copy of the Agreement and may obtain a fresh copy from the Personnel Department.

10   COMMENCEMENT AND TERMINATION OF AGREEMENT

This Agreement comes into force from 2 June 1966. Should any party wish to terminate this Agreement, six clear months' notice in writing of such intention and the reason for the intention shall be given by one party to the others.